blobitecture

blobitecture

John K Waters   Waveform architecture and digital design

GLOUCESTER MASSACHUSETTS

ROCKPORT PUBLISHERS

First published in the United States of America by **Rockport** Publishers, Inc.
33 Commercial Street,
Gloucester, Massachusetts 01930-5089
Telephone: (978) 282-9590
Fax: (978) 283-2742
www.rockpub.com

Library of Congress Cataloging-in-Publication Data
Waters, John K. (John Kevin)
    Blobitecture: Waveform architecture and digital
    design/John K. Waters
        p.   cm
    ISBN 1-59253-000-1 (paper over board)
    1. Organic architecture—Computer-aided design. I. Title.
NA682.073W36 2003
721'09'045—dc21   2003008831
                                                           CIP

ISBN 1-59253-000-1

10 9 8 7 6 5 4 3 2 1

Design: Wilson Harvey: London
Cover Image: Clockwise: Courtesy of Greg Lynn FORM,
Mark Laita/Apple Computer, Inc., Courtesy of Umbra,
Courtesy of Volkswagen of America

Printed in China

To Alex, Elizabeth, Rachel, and Sam; Sierra, Mackenzie, and Hunter; Jon and Tim; Alexis, Greg, and Mikey, from their **blobby** Uncle John.

contents

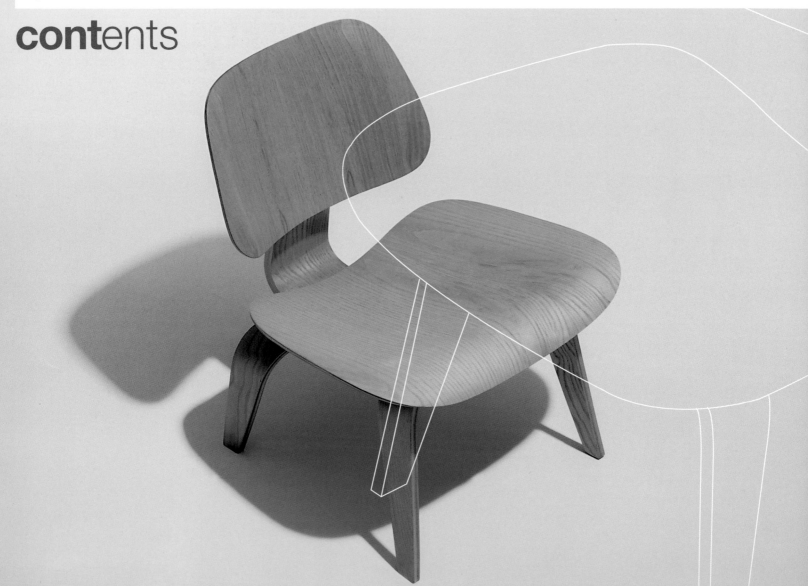

introduction

metaclay, metaballs, and **blobs**

Computers have played an essential role in the practice of architecture and industrial design for decades. But during the mid-1990s, some practitioners began setting aside traditional computer-aided design (CAD) systems to experiment with the more sophisticated 3-D modeling programs used for movie special effects and animation. They discovered that the essentially unlimited ability of these programs to stretch, fold, and distort three-dimensional forms in virtual space and to alter those forms with virtual forces, such as weight and motion, made them extraordinarily powerful tools of artistic expression and exploration. Working with virtual structures called isomorphic polysurfaces—better known among techies as "meta-clay," "metaballs," or simply **"blobs"**—they created fluid forms that were beyond the capabilities of CAD programs and that previous generations of drawing-board-bound designers could only have imagined.

When architecture critic Reed Kroloff saw early examples of the organically globular structures that emerged from these explorations, he recognized a new genre aborning and christened it **"blobitecture."** The computer-generated, digitally evolved structures of this new genre were "less built than born," observed Mark Dery in *I.D.* magazine. The architect-theorist most closely identified with the new genre, Greg Lynn, called his work **"blob architecture"** and talked about "the evolution of a form and its shaping forces." Lynn even invoked the image of the capital "B" **Blob**—the rippling mass of red Jell-O that oozed after a callow Steve McQueen in the 1958 film, *The Blob*—to explain his new "paradigm for an aqueous, alien structure."

Working in virtual environments beyond the world of Platonic solids and Cartesian planes, where space enfolds and objects become "soft," Lynn and others could generate models that transcended fixed frameworks, and evolve improbably plastic and flexible structures and objects. In an environment inhabited by forms that resembled malleable and obedient B-movie monsters, forms that Lynn called "fluid entities" and "quasi-solids," architecture was no longer static, but a "participant

The oozing B-movie monster of the 1950s represents **blobitecture's** "paradigm for an aqueous, alien structure."

immersed within dynamic flows."

What emerged from those dynamic flows could only be described with biological metaphors: a museum with layered and luminous "skin," a private residence with walls that functioned as "thermo-dynamic organs," built-in furnishings that "gastrulated" from the floors and walls, housing units that "evolved" via "genetic manipulation," a public edifice that resembled a "giant testicle."

Some industrial designers used the technology to spawn similarly biomorphic designs: "torso" shopping bags, womblike office cubicles, jellyfish barstools, "kissing" salt-and-pepper shakers. With the tools to render virtually any conceivable bump, wrinkle, or fold and the means to see those ripples re-created in the real world through the wonders of computer-aided manufacturing technologies and wondrously pliable new materials, these designers engaged in a kind of **blobization** of everyday things.

But the computer-generated designs that came to be called **blobitecture**—including **blob** architecture and **blobist** industrial

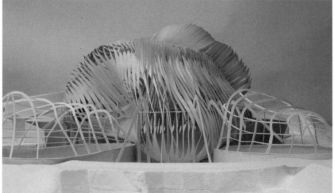

Greg Lynn's conceptual Embryological House evolved in a virtual environment where space enfolds and objects become "soft."

design—represented more than merely a generation of lumpy buildings and squishy furniture. The evolving capabilities of the tools themselves were challenging long-standing notions about architecture and design—or at least they were making such a challenge unavoidable.

Moreover, these computer generated forms signaled an important shift in the relationship between the designer and the computer. The computer was already the tool of the trade in many, if not most, architectural practices and design firms, both because of its power to boost efficiencies and its extraordinary versatility as an artistic instrument. But now, for some, it began to work almost as a collaborator. Architects like Lynn and industrial designers like Karim Rashid, who coined the term **"blobject,"** were using these technologies not merely to render and refine their ideas but to discover new things about them.

Some of the architects and designers discussed in these pages embraced the **blob**; others reacted against it. They all used emerging technologies to create innovative and complex designs that could not be ignored and that challenged established notions. And I believe that their work and ideas are still transforming architecture and industrial design.

My goals in this book are both grand and modest: to report on the labors of architects and designers who I have worked in and around these virtual spaces, and to look at the technologies they have used to get there. Readers won't find an encyclopedia of **blobitecture** in these pages, but instead a somewhat historical look at **blob** architecture and **blobject** design.

I make no attempt to cover every influence and "ism," or to include every architect or designer who ever devised a bump or bulge.

But I believe that the big links are here: the post-WWII biomorphic impulses of Eero Saarinen, Russel Wright, and the Eameses; the boundary busting buildings of Frank Gehry; the animate architectures of Lynn; and the sensuous **blobjects** of Rashid. Readers will find Embryological House, Big Sky, and "Fred and Ginger;" the iMac, the New Beetle, and the Palm V. They'll find **Blobby** Objects and NURBs; the Globject and the **Superblob**; toroids, electronic fauna, and chimeras; "the evolution of a form and its shaping forces" and "design dissolving into behavior." They'll find the "fluid dimensionless territories" of architects whose designs bridge the physical and digital worlds. They'll find a wastebasket that has become a design icon. They'll even find an **anti-blob**.

Where all of this is leading isn't exactly clear (to me at any rate), and I refrain from speculating in these pages. Some design and architecture watchers with no aversion to prognostication have suggested that the **blob** is already oozing from the scene; some say the invasion of the **blob** has just begun. What should be clear to anyone, however, is that the technologies that spawned these improbably fluid forms are here to stay, and the people who use them to design the spaces in which we live, work, and play, as well as the objects with which we fill those spaces, have just begun to explore their potential to shape our world.

Postwar architects and designers rage against the machine age

Eero Saarinen's Gateway Arch in St. Louis, Missouri, is a tapered curve of stainless steel 630 feet (192 meters) wide at its base and rising 630 feet (192 meters) above the St. Louis skyline.

The computer-generated designs that came to be called **"blobitecture"**—including for the purposes of this book, **blob** architecture and **blobist** industrial design—didn't begin appearing until the 1990s. But within an earlier generation of architects and designers, there were those who managed to inform their works with a similar organic aesthetic without the help of high-tech tools. In fact, although this group embraced a range of new materials, from plastics and fiber-glass to molded plywood, many of the irregular structures and curvilinear compositions they produced during the 1940s, 1950s, and 1960s were, at least in part, a reaction against technology.

In a 2002 interview with Doug Stewart for *Smithsonian* magazine, Kevin Stayton, curator of decorative arts at the Brooklyn Museum of Art, characterized this trend as a rejection of "Machine Age forms," if not an out and out denunciation of the "skyscrapers and streamlined

birth of the **blob**

objects that celebrated the machine." It was, Stayton suggested, a reaction against the engines of warfare. "The war didn't make the machine look like such a salvation after all…" he said.

These postwar designers and architects drew their inspiration from nature, and manifested their anti-machine impulses in designs for buildings and objects that were, if not strictly **blobs**, certainly more biological than prevailing styles.

Sculptural forms and curvaceous concrete

The curving contours and swooping walls of Finnish architect Eero Saarinen's TWA Terminal Buildings at New York's John F. Kennedy Airport (known as Idlewild Airport when the buildings were completed in 1962) have led architecture critics to consider it one of the icons of postwar biomorphic architecture. The terminal's molded concrete interior in which the staircases, check-in desk, and seating seemed to flow into the floors and walls, was almost more sculpture than architecture. Sylvia Hart Wright, author of *Sourcebook of Contemporary North American Architecture: From Postwar to Postmodern* (Van Nostrand Reinhold, 1989), has described the terminal as a "…blend of graceful sculptural forms selected to suggest the excitement of the trip." In his *Twentieth Century Architecture: A Visual History* (Facts on File, Inc., 1991), Dennis Sharp called the terminal "…One of the most self-assured, self-confident—even self-conscious—buildings to emerge as a result of the interplay of the architectonic and engineer-inspired buildings…. Its birdlike symbolism, exciting forms and cavernous interior were… a demonstration of the architect's role as an originator and, in the American scene, as a 'building stylist'.…"

Saarinen is probably better known for another curvilinear design: his Gateway Arch in St. Louis, Missouri. Designed in 1947

Charles and Ray Eames's experiments with molded plywood lead to the development of their famous "potato chip chair."

and completed in 1966, the memorial arch is a tapered curve of stainless steel 630 feet (192 meters) wide at its base and rising 630 feet (192 meters) above the St. Louis skyline. Saarinen's simple, towering arch, the tallest such structure in the United States, became known as the "Gateway to the West."

Saarinen originally studied sculpture, which is not surprising. A clearly sculptural sensibility informs much of his work. In 1959, he talked with authors Peter Gossel and Gabriele Leuthauser (*Architecture in the Twentieth Century*, Taschen America Llc, 1999) about the TWA Terminal. "All the curves, all the spaces and elements right down to the shape of the signs, display boards, railings and check-in desks were to be of a matching nature," he said. "We wanted passengers passing through the building to experience a fully designed environment, in which each part arises from another and everything belongs to the same formal world."

Even the legendary Frank Lloyd Wright showed a decidedly biomorphic bent near the end of his career. His landmark Guggenheim Museum in New York, completed in 1959 and one of the last of Wright's designs to be realized, is a curvaceous concrete structure situated across from Central Park on the city's 5th Avenue Museum Mile. Much like Saarinen's TWA Terminal, the result is sculptural. The building's most striking feature is a circular ramp gallery, which Spiro Kostof described in his *A History of Architecture, Settings and Rituals* (Oxford University Press, 1985) as a "continuous spatial helix, a circular ramp that expands as it coils vertiginously around an unobstructed well of space capped by a flat-ribbed glass dome…"

Wright called his Guggenheim design an "optimistic ziggurat" that evoked for him "the quiet unbroken wave." For Wright, the design was aesthetically successful, but also eminently practical. Explaining his thinking about the museum to *The Architectural Forum* in 1948, he said, "Entering into the spirit of this interior, you will discover the best possible atmosphere in which to show fine paintings or listen to music. It is this atmosphere that seems to me most lacking in our art galleries, museums, music halls and theaters."

The most striking feature of Wright's Guggenheim Museum in New York is an interior, circular ramp gallery, which has been described as a "continuous spatial helix." The ramp expands as it coils around an unobstructed well of space capped by a flat-ribbed glass dome.

Legendary architect Frank Lloyd Wright gave his landmark Guggenheim Museum in New York a curvaceous concrete structure. Wright's "optimistic ziggurat" is strikingly sculptural and somewhat biomorphic, if not precisely **blobist**.

Wright was not known for designs that were organic, per se, but rather for long, low buildings with hovering planes that emphasized the horizontal. Called prairie houses, these buildings were developed around the basic crucifix, L, or T shape—a decidedly **unbloblike** blueprint. But neither was Wright trapped in the traditional box. He originated the idea of "defined" as opposed to "enclosed" interior spaces. Rejecting the notion that rooms were merely single-function cubes, he created overlapping and interpenetrating rooms with shared spaces.

Perhaps the **blobiest** architect of the postwar era was the flamboyant Morris Lapidus, best known as the designer of gaudy and glamorous resort hotels in South Florida. During his 60-year career, Lapidus designed more than 500 retail stores, hotels, apartment complexes, and stage sets. He was a well-established retail designer when he built his first hotel in 1954, the Fontainebleau in Miami Beach. He went on to design the Eden Roc in 1955, and the Americana in 1956. (The Americana is now the Sheraton Bal Harbour.)

Lapidus's background as a set and costume designer for theater showed in his architecture, which combined French Provincial and Italian Romanesque styles with whimsical ornamentation and an unrestrained use of color. His buildings were curvy and sensual, and his interiors were filled with dramatic lighting and amorphous forms.

His interior design elements were distinctly biomorphic, and all his own. The backlit cutout openings that dotted the curved walls he called "cheese holes;" amoeboid cutouts that hung like dropped ceilings or adorned carpets he dubbed "woggles;" and exposed floor-to-ceiling supports were "beanpoles." The architect has characterized his work as a banquet of delight and joy. He once told an interviewer, "If you like ice cream, why stop with one scoop; have three scoops, too much is never enough. Enjoy! Enjoy!"

During most of his career, the critics, who favored Ludwig Mies van der Rohe's International Style, hated Lapidus's work, and they shunned him. A 1960 *Time* magazine article called him "a disciple of excess." In his 1996 memoir, *Too Much Is Never Enough* (Rizzoli, 1996), Lapidus recalled his rejection by the establishment: "The critics, they just not only didn't like my work, they couldn't say enough horrible things about me," he wrote. "I was never published for over 30 years in any architectural book or magazine. I was anathema."

Lapidus's contributions to architecture were eventually recognized. Among other awards and acknowledgements, he was named an American Original by the Smithsonian Institution's Cooper-Hewitt, National Design Museum in its first national design awards.

Despite the anti-machine aesthetic of the postwar designers, it was in large measure the materials developed by the "war machine" that allowed them to innovate. Wartime manufacturing fueled the rapid development of new materials, such as fiberglass; plastics like nylon (invented by Dupont in 1939); polyethylene and polyester (1942); processed woods, such as plywood, which was used in warplanes; and metal alloys.

Plastic in particular made possible the realization of fluid forms and organic shapes. Perhaps the **blobiest** building to emerge from this period was nearly all plastic: the Monsanto House of the Future, a rounded, concept house first exhibited at Disneyland Park's Tomorrowland in Orlando, Florida, in 1957.

Looking for all the world like a massive, white mushroom, sliced open to accommodate two picture windows, the Monsanto House was designed by the architecture department at the Massachusetts Institute of Technology, built by the Monsanto Company, and opened to the public on a prime section of Disneyland real estate. The structure's frame was 100 percent plastic, according to Monsanto, and weighed nearly 15,000 pounds (6,804 kilograms). Though dominated by plastics, the interior also included textiles, glass, bronze, and other materials.

Disney's Monsanto House was designed by the architecture department at the Massachusetts Institute of Technology and built by the Monsanto Company in 1957. The structure's frame was 100 percent plastic and weighed nearly 15,000 pounds.

Charles and Ray Eames were among the most innovative industrial designers of the post-war period. Their use of new materials, such as the molded plywood in their famous "potato chip chair" and this coffee table, allowed them to create furniture with soft, irregular curves and biomorphic shapes inspired by nature.

Another markedly sculptural building, the Monsanto House had four wings cantilevered off a central pedestal and extending over a garden. Within the four wings were the curved walls and cambered ceilings of a living room, family room, kitchen, dining room, three bedrooms, and two baths. More than 20 million visitors toured the house, which featured such innovations as insulated glass walls; picture telephones; large, flat, wall-mounted televisions; microwave ovens; foam-backed plastic floor coverings; speaker phones; and a brand new innovation, the electric toothbrush.

The house stood at the entrance to Disneyland Park's Tomorrowland until it was deemed too "old fashioned" in 1967. According to Monsanto, the demolition, which was planned for one day, ended up taking two weeks, because the wrecking ball just bounced off the building's plastic walls. Workers reportedly resorted to cutting the house to pieces with hacksaws.

Potato chip chairs and glowing **blobs**

Pliable new materials also allowed an organic vocabulary to emerge in the field of industrial design. Furniture, for example, began to take on soft, irregular curves and biomorphic shapes inspired by nature. In 1940, architect Eero Saarinen collaborated with Charles Eames to design a revolutionary body-molded plywood shell chair. Organic Chair won first prize in a competition at the Museum of Modern Art. In fact, the two architects collaborated on a series of furniture that dominated the "Organic Design in Home Furnishings" show at the MoMA that year, including the chair, a sofa unit, and wooden shelving and desk furniture.

Saarinen experimented with molded plywood, working with Charles and Ray Eames under the auspices of their Plyformed Products Company. During the 1940s, they created splints for the United States Navy designed to conform to the contours of the human body, and they applied these same processes in their designs of plywood furniture.

In the late 1940s, Saarinen designed a number of biomorphic chairs for Knoll Associates. His famous Womb Chair, created in 1946, was a molded and upholstered shell set in a steel-rod cradle frame. It was designed to envelop the sitter, allowing him or her to curl up within it in comfort. Explaining his design, Saarinen once said, "People sit differently today than they did in the Victorian era. They sit lower and they like to slouch.... The Womb Chair... also attempts to achieve a psychological comfort by providing a great big cuplike shell into which you can curl up and pull up your legs."

Saarinen's Tulip Chair consisted of a shell of molded fiberglass perched on a pedestal base of cast aluminum. Disappointed that the technology of the time would not permit him to make the chair out of a single, continuous piece of plastic, he painted the base to match the shell and give that impression. The Tulip Chair was one of a number of pedestal pieces Saarinen designed to clean up the "slum of legs" in domestic interiors. About the design, Saarinen has written:

The bases of tables and chairs in a typical furniture arrangement create an ugly, confusing, and restless world. I wanted to design a chair as an integrated whole once again. All important furniture of the past always had a holistic structure, from King Tut's chair to that of Thomas Chippendale. Today, we are parting ways with this holism with our predilection for plastic and laminated wood shells. I am looking forward to the point when the plastics industry will be capable of manufacturing the chair using just one material, the way I have designed it.

While Saarinen designed for Knoll, Charles Eames went on to design for Herman Miller, and to an even more important collaboration. The work of the husband-and-wife design team of Charles and Ray Eames evinces a striking organic aesthetic. Charles, who was trained as an architect, and Ray, who was trained as a painter, combined their disciplines and made a prolific design duo. From the 1940s to the 1970s, they designed furniture, buildings, exhibitions, interiors, toys, books, and graphics. They even made films.

But it is their furniture designs for which they are most often remembered. By applying innovative uses of the new materials and technologies developed during the war, they changed mass production of contemporary furniture. Their experiments with molded plywood led to the development of their famous "potato chip chair." Working at home in their Venice, California, apartment in the early 1940s, the Eameses tested wood-molding techniques using thin sheets of wood veneer and bicycle pumps as compressors.

The original Eames Lounge Wood Chair was unveiled in 1946. It consisted of rounded pieces of five-ply molded plywood bent into body-friendly compound curves. It had hardwood inner plies and light ash face veneers, all coated with either a clear or an ebony finish.

Designed by Charles and Ray Eames, this molded plywood folding screen has a sculpted, undulating form consisting of six curved wood sections. The Herman Miller Company still sells the screens.

The popularity of the Eames's molded plywood chair was all but unprecedented. Herman Miller continues to produce the chairs today. A version with metal tube legs sells for $420, and an all-wood version goes for $716. Sold at auction, the originals can now go for tens of thousands of dollars. The chair has appeared consistently on many "best of" design lists of the 20th century.

The Eameses also designed a molded plywood coffee table with a slightly indented top and gently curved legs. The Eames's molded plywood folding screen had a sculpted, undulating form consisting of six curved wood sections. According to the Herman Miller Company, which still sells the screens, the sections were joined by canvas hinges and a synthetic adhesive developed during World War II. Today a durable woven polypropylene mesh connects the sections.

Their elliptical table, nicknamed the "surfboard table" for its long (89 inches [226 centimeters]) lean contours, was designed in the early 1950s. Sold initially from 1951 to 1964, the table was reissued by Herman Miller for the home in 1994.

The table's wire base was one result of the Eameses' experimentation with bent and welded wire. That work also produced a variety of experimental pieces, including their Wire Mesh Chair. According to author Pat Kirkham, the chair's double-wire edging received the first American mechanical patent for design. In his book, *Charles and Ray Eames: Designers of the Twentieth Century* (MIT Press 1998), Kirkham writes: "The wire mesh chair, an exemplary essay on the minimal use of a 'new' material, had a tremendous impact." Once in production, the chair found its way into offices, hotels, and restaurants around the country.

The Eames's experimented extensively with bent and welded wire, producing a number of experimental pieces, including their Wire Mesh Chair. The chair's double-wire edging received the first American mechanical patent for design. Once in production, the chair found its way into offices, hotels, and restaurants around the country.

The Eames's famous "surfboard table," named for its elliptical shape, combined a curvilinear wood top with a wire base, which was one result of the their experimentation with bent and welded wire.

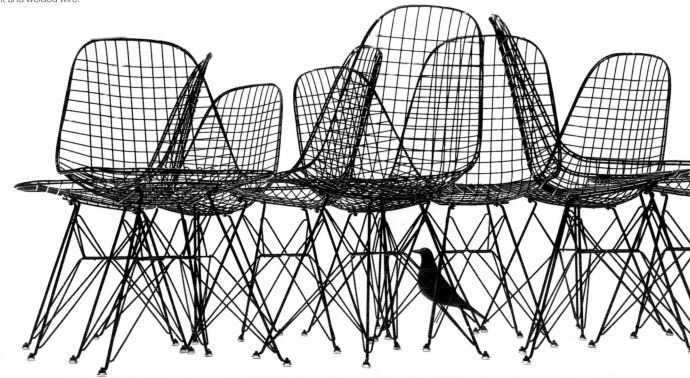

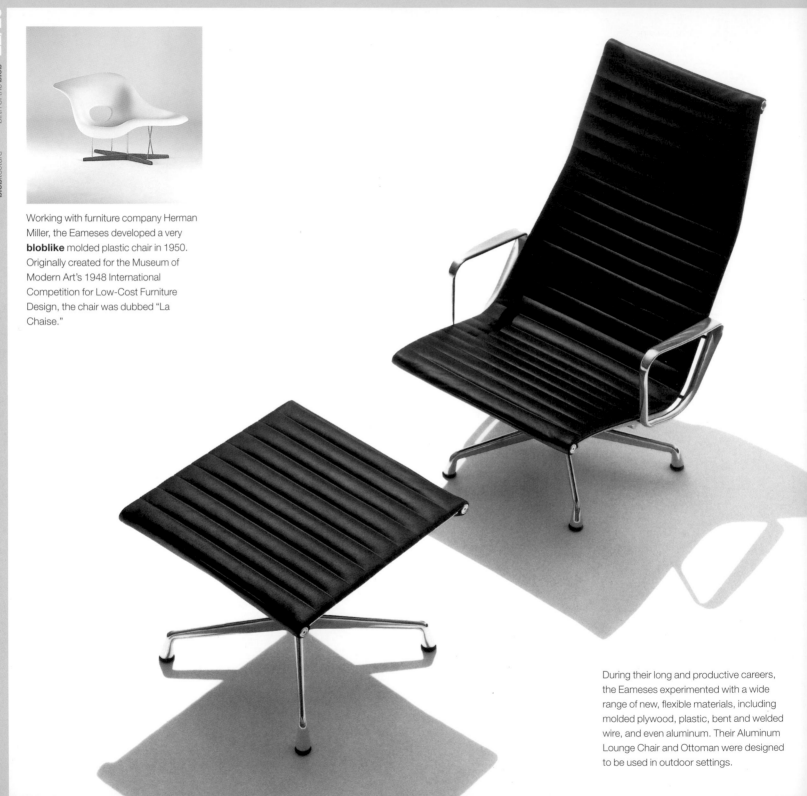

Working with furniture company Herman Miller, the Eameses developed a very **bloblike** molded plastic chair in 1950. Originally created for the Museum of Modern Art's 1948 International Competition for Low-Cost Furniture Design, the chair was dubbed "La Chaise."

During their long and productive careers, the Eameses experimented with a wide range of new, flexible materials, including molded plywood, plastic, bent and welded wire, and even aluminum. Their Aluminum Lounge Chair and Ottoman were designed to be used in outdoor settings.

Plastic was, of course, another new material that had a tremendous impact on postwar designers, and the Eameses were no exception. Working with Herman Miller, the Eameses developed a very **bloblike** molded plastic chair in 1950. Created for the 1948 International Competition for Low-Cost Furniture Design, sponsored by the Museum of Modern Art, the chair was dubbed La Chaise, both as homage to sculptor Gaston Lachaise, whose Floating Figure sculpture inspired the design, and as a pun on his name.

According to Pat Kirkham, the Eameses found the original chair material (fiberglass cloth and plastic resin) in military-surplus shops. They had used for screens in their home. This material eventually evolved into the high-impact plastic used in the production of the chairs today, according to Herman Miller.

The glass-top coffee table designed by artist Isamu Noguchi in 1947 is another early example of organic forms in furniture design. A gently curved wooden base of natural or ebonized walnut supports the ovoid glass top. Noguchi was a sculptor, designer, architect, and craftsman. His belief that sculpture could lead us to a better understanding of man's struggle with nature informed all of his work. "Everything is sculpture," Noguchi once said. "Any material, any idea without hindrance born into space, I consider sculpture."

During his long career, Noguchi's created abstract sculpture, designed stage sets and furniture, planned parks and playgrounds, and conceive monuments. In the 1940s he designed furniture for Herman Miller. His coffee table caught the company's attention when George

Nelson, Herman Miller's head designer, used his design for the piece to illustrate an article. Nelson was, himself, responsible for the development of an innovative line of furniture for the company. He also commissioned new designs from others. His first commission was Noguchi's coffee table.

About his celebrated coffee table, Noguchi has written:

There was the time I went to Hawaii in 1939 to do an advertisement (with Georgia O'Keefe). As a result of this I had met Robsjohn Gibbings, the furniture designer, who had asked me to do a coffee table for him. (I had already done a table for Conger Goodyear.) I designed a small model in plastic and heard no further before I went west. While interned in Boston I was surprised to see a variation of this published

Artist Isamu Noguchi's iconic glass-top coffee table, designed in 1947, is another example of organic forms in furniture design from the postwar period. Noguchi saw his furniture designs as sculpture, which he believed could lead us to a better understanding of man's struggle with nature.

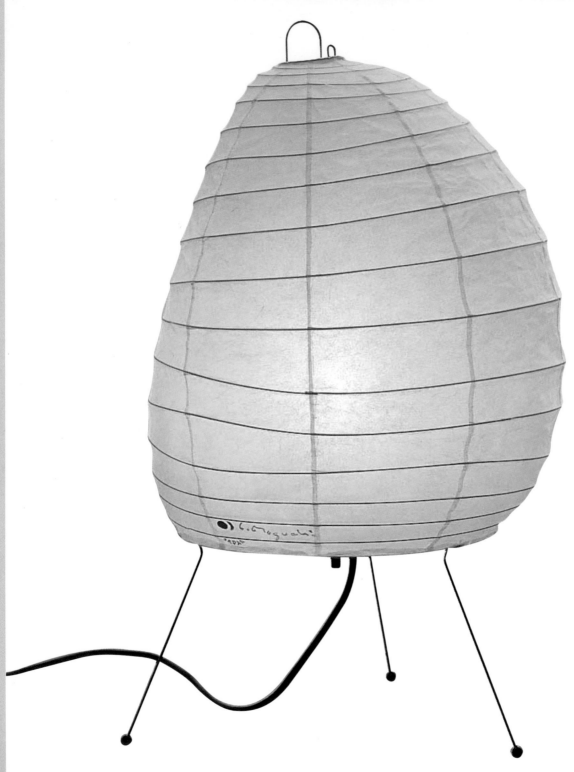

Noguchi's renowned Akari lamps exhibit an unmistakable organic sensibility. Considered by the artist to be "light sculptures," and inspired by traditional Japanese paper lanterns, they are constructed of mulberry bark and bamboo, incorporating not only an organic form factor but organic materials.

as a Gibbings advertisement. When, on my return I remonstrated, he said anybody could make a three-legged table. In revenge, I made my own variant of my own table, articulated as the Goodyear table, but reduced to rudiments. It illustrated an article by George Nelson called "How to make a table."

Nelson was also responsible for bringing the designs of Charles Eames to Herman Miller, according to the company, and he collaborated with R. Buckminster Fuller on a number of projects. His own creations—his Bubble Lamp, Ball Clock, and Marshmallow Sofa—should certainly be counted among the designs prefiguring **blobitecture**.

Noguchi created a number of organic pieces for Herman Miller, including a wood-and-metal "rudder" dining table and stools, as well as a free-form sofa and companion piece. Herman Miller reissued his glass-top coffee table in 1984.

Another Noguchi design, his renowned Akari lamps, exhibit an unmistakable organic sensibility.

Considered by the artist to be "light sculptures," and inspired by traditional Japanese paper lanterns, they are constructed of mulberry bark and bamboo, thus incorporating not only an organic form factor but organic materials. Intended to embody pure light and weightlessness, the lamps are nothing if not glowing **blobs**.

Harry Bertoia was another sculptor who ventured into furniture design. The Italian-born artist joined the Eameses in their California studio in 1943, where he designed furniture and contributed to their work on molded plywood. Later, he developed a line of metal furniture for Knoll. His famous wire chairs were conceived as functional sculptures comprising a network of small diamond patterns within a large diamond shape. The chairs came with various types of optional fabric covers that hooked onto the frames.

Bertoia, who was also a painter, printmaker, and jewelry maker, has said that his Diamond Chair grew out of a sculptural aesthetic. His aim was to create airily transparent

Another artist turned furniture designer, Italian-born Harry Bertoia worked with the Eameses in their California studio in 1943. Bertoia's celebrated wire chairs were conceived as functional sculptures comprising a network of small diamond patterns within a large diamond shape.

Bertoia's wire chair designs included his Bird Chair, which was made entirely by hand in wooden wire-bending frames, and has been in continuous production since the 1950s.

shapes floating in space. Looking at the skeletal grid work of his chairs, he wrote, one could see that "space passes through them."

Bertoia's wire chairs appeared in 1952, about a year after some wire chairs designed by the Eameses. The series included his Diamond Chair, Bird Chair (presumably a chicken wire reference), a wider version of the Diamond Chair called a Wide Diamond, a set of barstools, side chairs without arms, and smaller versions of the side chairs designed for children. Most of these pieces have been in continuous production since the 1950s, made entirely by hand in wooden wire-bending frames.

Zoomorphic spoons and sharky sports cars

Postwar designers of even the most commonplace objects found inspiration in organic shapes and patterns. The dinnerware, glassware, ceramics, fine china, and cutlery they created reflected this biomorphic trend.

Among industrial designers of the 1940s and 50s, no name is better known than Russel Wright. In fact, his is the first true designer brand name, beating the likes of Martha Stewart and Ralph Lauren to the punch by decades. Wright was a "Quaker-born child of privilege" who began designing in the era of Deco and Bauhaus, although he never really aligned himself with either school. Wright designed tablecloths, cutlery, glassware, pottery, and furniture. His dinnerware was designed to go from stove to table. He created the first sectional couch.

Wright's widely collected designs relied on simple patterns of line and sensuous zoomorphic curves. Even his colors were muted and organic: nutmeg, lettuce, pink sherbet, and apricot. He designed pitchers in spun aluminum. His Oceana line of wood serving pieces, created in 1935, included a rosette casual serving tray with snail-like spiral furrows. His Oceana centerpiece was all squiggles and ripples. His Iroquois Casual China carafes, designed in 1946, were distinctly gourdlike jugs rendered in organic hues.

In 1939, Wright introduced his celebrated American Modern glazed-ceramic dinnerware collection. According to Ann Kerr, author of the *Collector's Encyclopedia of Russel Wright* (Collector Books, 2002), that collection would become the best-selling dinnerware of all time, grossing $159 million over its 20-year production span.

Another widely collected industrial designer of that period, Eva Zeisel, created everyday dinnerware for Sears, Roebuck & Co., as well as fine china for Red Wing, Castleton, and Hall. The Hungarian-born Zeisel's work in the 1930s and '40s relied on geometrical forms, but she communicated the postwar biomor-

Auto designer Harley Earl gave us chrome bumpers and tail fins, and introduced the practice of modeling auto-design prototypes in three dimensions with clay. He also gave us the smooth, organic curves of the Corvette, which was introduced by General Motors in the early 1950s.

phic impulse perfectly in 1946 with her Town and Country dinner service, which featured her now famous amoeboid salt-and-pepper shakers.

Considered one of America's greatest ceramic and industrial designers, Zeisel's works were mass-produced in the United States, and many are in permanent collections in major museums. In 2001, the then 94-year-old designer told Karen E. Steen in an interview for *Metropolis* magazine, that she saw her work as "the playful search for beauty."

The postwar organic repudiation of the Machine Age even managed to influence designers of the machine that shaped postwar America: the automobile. Newly available plastics and fiberglass made it possible to infuse vehicle design with a genuinely biomorphic sensibility.

The molded organic shape of the Corvette, for example, which was introduced by General Motors in the early 1950s, was facilitated by the use of fiberglass and plastics. The brainchild of auto industry legend Harley Earl, the Corvette was and is considered *the* American sports car. Named for a swift naval vessel from

World War II, it made its public debut at the 1953 New York Motorama at the Waldorf-Astoria hotel.

Earl had gone to work for GM in 1927, supervising the automaker's newly created Art and Color Section, which would evolve into the GM Design and Styling Department. By the time he retired in 1958, that department had grown from a staff of 50 to 1,100. During the course of his career, Earl introduced chrome, two-tone paint, tail fins, hardtops, and wrap-around windshields to the automotive design palette.

Earl introduced curves, chrome, and tail fins with his 1948 Cadillac design, and repeated these elements in his 1950 Le Sabre and numerous vehicles designed and built throughout the 1950s and early '60s. He drew from the design of aircraft, but he was also greatly inspired by the grace and aerodynamics of sharks.

Earl also introduced the practice of modeling auto-design prototypes in three dimensions with clay. The practice lacked the flexibility provided by 3-D modeling software linked with computer numerical control technologies used by

designers today, but it was highly innovative at the time, and it brought an equally sculptural sensibility to the work.

Some have even argued that the postwar biomorphic design sensibility was responsible for such pop-culture artifacts as the Slinky, the hula-hoop, bright-and-bulgy jukeboxes, and the kidney shaped pools that were all the rage during the 1950s. (Even Elvis had one.) They may be right; at some point, style propagates for its own sake. Who can say how deeply the organic forms favored by postwar designers and architects influenced the designers of telephones, typewriters, and tape dispensers, regardless of the utility of such forms. Perhaps the ultimate example of this influence was a chair that appeared in 1968. Italian designers Piero Gatti, Cesare Paolini, and Franco Teodoro unveiled their malleable, minimalist, polystyrene-pellet-filled bag (originally leather) that year. They called it Il Sacco, but this quintessential **blob**, which became a fixture in college dorm rooms across America, was better known as the beanbag chair.

chapter 2
blob's your uncle

Frank O. Gehry shows a generation how to design beyond the box

Architect Frank O. Gehry's Guggenheim Museum in Bilbao, Spain, departs radically from the traditional white cube of museum architecture. Its undulating curves and irregular geometries are clad in one-third-inch-thick (8.4mm) titanium panels.

The biomorphic structures and organic designs referred to as **"blobitecture"** have their roots in the postmodernist rebellion against the perceived mechanistic dryness of modernism, with its well-known emphasis on function, scientific analysis, and order. It was a fruitful revolt, but the results are not easily categorized. Postmodernist architecture is sometimes seen to be, as the website Art and Culture (www.artandculture.com) puts it, "…one of the most vague and deliberately elusive concepts in recent architectural practice…." What best-selling author, architect, and maven of postmodernism, Charles Jencks, calls "this disparate tradition," encompasses a host of isms, from contextualism to radical eclecticism—and, it appears, **blobism**.

A host of names come up when talk turns to postmodernist architecture: Robert Venturi, Nigel Coates, Rem Koolhaas, Peter Eisenman (for whom leading **blobitecture** theorist Greg Lynn worked), Michael Graves, and many others. But perhaps the most direct link to **blobitecture** may be seen in the works of Frank Gehry, whose formally fragmented spaces and nonorthogonal forms anticipate the space-folding, biomorphic approaches of the **blobists**.

"In Gehry, we see the idea of adding nature," observes Bill Moggridge, principal at the renowned industrial design firm, IDEO. "Natural forms become a rich part of the inspiration. It wasn't just postmodernism. This was a new kind of movement, which is really the origin of what is called **blobitecture** in my head. You could call it **blobitecture** or natural in terms of its influence from the forms you find in nature."

The organic, earthy contours of his highly emotional designs notwithstanding, architect Frank O. Gehry's preference for sketches on paper and handmade models might seem to put him at odds with the technology-driven design methodologies of the digitized crowd. But Gehry, who does utilize advanced computer technology as part of his design process, has been called the **blobist's** "professional uncle."

Digital interpreter
Gehry is arguably the world's most famous architect. Only the late Frank Lloyd Wright has greater public name recognition. Gehry's long and productive career bridges the postwar and current generations of designers and architects. Over the years he has designed libraries, office buildings, restaurants, schools, private residences, visual and performing arts venues, exhibition spaces, and furniture. In 1989, when Gehry won the Pritzker Prize, a lifetime achievement award commonly referred to as the "Nobel of architecture," *New York Times* architecture critic Paul Goldberger wrote, "Gehry's buildings are powerful essays in geometric form and materials, and from an aesthetic standpoint they are among the most profound and brilliant works of architecture of our time."

Gehry's design process typically begins with simple sketches, which evolve into paper and cardboard models. He is known to work simultaneously on two or three versions in different scales. Although he has characterized modeling as a "trivial" but necessary part of the process, his Santa Monica, California-based architecture studio maintains a staff of more than 60, including model-making specialists with access to extensive model-making facilities.

Gehry doesn't often use computers to devise his designs, but he eventually turns to technology to work out how to build them. Through the implementation of a network of sophisticated CAD workstations, his cardboard models are scanned, mapped, and reborn in the virtual space of a 3-D digital design program.

Gehry's practice famously pioneered the use in architecture of a sophisticated computer design program originally intended for an entirely different purpose. Called

CATIA (Computer-Aided Three-Dimensional Interactive Application), the program was developed some 20 years ago by Dassault Systemes of France as a design tool for the French aviation and aerospace industries. CATIA is a complex, 3-D, numeric-surface-and-solids-modeling program that Gehry and company use extensively to refine and manage the complex wall and roof structures and unconventional building materials typical of their designs.

In CATIA, each 3-D component—say, a single airplane wing—represents a unified database that can analyze fabrication, aerodynamics, surface stresses, hydraulics, electronics, temperature gradients, geometries of compound curves, and potential interferences between cross-connections. In other words, the 3-D models generated in CATIA can be used to produce "bending moments," shear forces, and reactions due to loading conditions—exactly the kind of information Gehry needs to realize his idiosyncratic geometries.

Gehry's willingness to turn this engineering software to his own purposes must resonate with architects like Greg Lynn, who found a place in their own digital toolboxes for applications intended for animators. In a case study published by CenitDesktop, one of the United Kingdom's leading suppliers of software and system solutions for engineers and the manufacturing industry, Gehry comments on his evolving relationship to computers and design software:

This technology provides a way for me to get closer to the craft. In the past, there were many layers between my rough sketch and the final building, and the feeling of the design could get lost before it reached the craftsman. It feels like I've been speaking a foreign language, and now, all of a sudden, the craftsman understands me. In this case, the computer is not dehumanizing; it's an interpreter.

During a 2000 visit to Gehry's Santa Monica, California, offices, architecture critic Giles Worsley had a chance to observe the architect's relationship with computers first hand. He shared his observations in the British *Telegraph*:

The process becomes clear on a tour round the office. Models are the key to Gehry's design process. Where most architects of his generation express themselves in drawing, Gehry's drawings are surprisingly crude, almost cartoonish scribbles. Instead, Gehry works out his designs in models. Simple rectangular blocks are used to work out the uses of the different spaces and their relation to each other… With the overall massing agreed, Gehry starts ripping up paper and sticking it over the models. Once a rough design has been reached, assistants turn it into a proper model, which Gehry alters again and again until the design is finalized. The last model is scanned into the computer and transformed into construction drawings. A big project, such as the large complex Gehry has just designed for MIT in Boston, will generate 250 to 300 models.

Gehry's Vitra International Manufacturing Facility and Design Museum in Weil am Rhein, Germany, was his first European commission. It marked a shift in his aesthetic toward more organic forms.

With his Experimental Edges collection
(1979–82), Gehry continued his foray
into furniture design. The cardboard
construction of these pieces featured
rough and shaggy edges.

An ongoing negotiation

Gehry's trailblazing in the digital design wilderness was a consequence, rather than a cause, of what has been called his "ongoing negotiation of functional architecture and sculptural form." Long before he began integrating computers into his design process—even before the advent of the personal computer—Gehry was thinking beyond the box.

In the late 1970s and early 1980s, Gehry's designs of private residences began to manifest his notion that "buildings under construction look nicer than buildings finished." His designs literally burst the box, rending the skin of wood-framed structures to reveal the bones beneath. His models for the unbuilt Wagner Residence and Familian Residence, for example, fragmented the buildings' outer layers and cocked traditional rectilinear forms into oblique angles, leaving windows and doors askew relative to the foundations.

During this period, Gehry's own Santa Monica, California, residence, an unassuming two-story house, provided the architect with a kind of laboratory in which he could experiment with untraditional spaces and idiosyncratic forms, as well as unconventional materials. Gehry gutted the interior, stripping the walls and ceilings down to their original two-by-four stud frames, beams, and rafters. He opened it further by installing large glass apertures rotated off square. He then expanded the structure by wrapping it in layers of corrugated aluminum metal siding and chain link, creating a new set of spaces around it.

The result was a kind of house within a house that blurred conventional ideas about "interior" and "exterior." As Paul Heyer observed in his *American Architecture: Ideas and Ideologies in the Late Twentieth Century* (Van Nostrand Reinhold, 1993), "…the effort here is cluttered expressionistic and the sensibility is freely intended as artistically intuitive, of accident not resolved. The palette is anti-high-tech in preference for a visual presence that is off the-shelf and ordinary 'cheap tech….' With the original house almost intact formwise, Gehry, in effect, lifted back the skin to reveal the building as layers, with new forms breaking out and tilting away from the original…."

Gehry's work on his Santa Monica home demonstrated his utter rejection of the modernist grid. It was for his kind of exploded building, and for his innovative use of cheap materials like chain-link fencing, corrugated iron, and roughly finished timber that he was first known.

Gehry's love of cheap materials was also apparent in his forays into furniture design. Exploring the possibilities of corrugated cardboard, for example, lead Gehry to create his Easy Edges collection (1969–73) of curvilinear tables and chairs. Gehry was very familiar with the material, because he used it to make many of his architectural models. But through experimentation he found that it could also provide a surprisingly sturdy and durable structure for furniture, especially when folded in piled curves and combined with a hardwood veneer. His Experimental Edges collection (1979–82), also of cardboard construction, featured rough, shaggy edges. The forms of his Bent Wood Furniture collection (1989–92), created for Knoll, were inspired by the bushel basket, and recall the sinuous folds of the Easy Edges line.

Gehry explored the potential of cheap materials, such as corrugated cardboard, in his furniture designs. In his Easy Edges collection (1969–73), he piled corrugated cardboard into hardwood-veneered curves and folds, creating surprisingly sturdy and durable chairs.

Fishy business

Interestingly, the first large-scale project for which Gehry utilized computer design software was not a building, but a piece of sculpture. He designed his Fish Sculpture at Vila Olimpica in 1985 for the 1992 Olympic games in Barcelona, Spain. The monumental 160-by-100-foot (49m x 30.5m) golden fish sculpture made of stone, steel, and glass, serves as a landmark and anchors a retail complex designed by Gehry within a larger Skidmore, Owings & Merrill hotel development.

A tight budget and a short dead-line reportedly led James M. Glymph, a partner in Gehry's firm, to search for a computer program that would speed things up by incorporating the design and construction process. He found CATIA's combination of design, manufacturing, and engineering capabilities to be the perfect solution. This marriage of design and manufacturing functionality would be enormously appealing to a later generation of architects. A modeler of complex surface geometries, CATIA analyzed data generated from the digitization of

physical models, which Gehry and company typically created, and the specifications drawn from that scan would be used directly to engineer and fabricate the components of Gehry's complex building systems.

The fish motif reappears in a number of Gehry's works. It first appeared in his unrealized design for the Smith Residence in 1981. He later designed a graceful, 70-foot-high (21.3m) fish sculpture made of chain link mesh for the Fishdance restaurant in Kobe, Japan, (1986–87); the mesh fish "dances" on its tail next to the main building. He developed his Fish and Snake Lamps in 1983 at the invitation of the Formica Company to show off a new laminate product called Colorcore. While he was working on the design, a model lamp was broken, leaving splintered patterns in the material. Gehry saw those patterns as scales, and worked them into his piscine designs, which emphasized the translucency of the material's integral coloration. New City Editions eventually produced nearly three dozen fish and snake lamps.

These projects underscore the

sculptural quality of much of Gehry's work. He once commented on his sculptural approach to architecture: "I don't know where you cross the line between architecture and sculpture. For me, it is the same. Buildings and sculpture are three-dimensional objects."

It has been suggested that it was Gehry's growing fascination with fish forms that softened the edges of the rigorously angular structures that characterized his early work. Gehry acknowledged this connection to the organic shift in his designs in an interview with Giles Worsley, "The fish was my attack on postmodernism," he said. "Postmodernism or the regurgitation of Greek temples is anthropomorphic, and I said, if you're going to go back, fish were here 300 million years before man, so why not use fish [as a model for architecture]? That's what I said in anger. Then I started drawing the damn thing and I realized something I was looking for . . . It was movement in an inert medium."

Architecture critic Joseph Giovannini saw Gehry's fish forms in his Vitra International Manufacturing

The fish motif reappears in a number of Gehry's works, including this beautiful example of one of his many fish lamps. Of his seeming obsession with the fish form, Gehry has said, "The fish was my attack on postmodernism."

Gehry developed his Fish and Snake Lamps in 1983 at the invitation of the Formica Company to show off a new laminate product called Colorcore. The splintered patterns in a broken model lamp looked like a pattern of scales to Gehry and inspired dozens of fish and snake lamps.

Facility and Design Museum (1987–89). Writing in *New York Magazine*, he observed that, in the Vitra design, Gehry "lops off the fish tail and head to develop the torso into turbulent abstractions."

Gehry's Vitra Facility in Weil-am-Rhein, Germany, was his first European commission, and it marked the shift in his aesthetic toward more organic forms. According to Vitra, Gehry was originally asked to come to Weil-am-Rhein in 1984 to help with the siting of a sculpture entitled "Balancing Tools" by Claes Oldenberg and Coosje van Bruggen. Gehry would later collaborate with the two artists on the whimsical Chiat/Day Building, which featured a façade made to look like a giant pair of binoculars. Gehry was also there to negotiate the re issue of his 1970's cardboard chair series, and he ended up talking with Vitra's chairman, Rolf Fehlbaum, about designing a building to house Vitra's extensive collection of modern furniture.

Gehry was eventually hired to design two buildings: the museum, which would house approximately 200 modern and contemporary chairs, and a factory for the Vitra furniture company. In the words of Gehry's firm, the resulting design "departed from the disparate layering of geometries and informal materials common to Gehry's southern California structures and evidences a shift toward more organically sculptural forms." The final, sloping, plaster-and-stucco structure consisted of Baroque arcs, undulating ramps, and gentle spirals that "imply collective movement, responding to the dynamic nature of the manufacturing center."

Vitra later commissioned Gehry to design the company's international headquarters building in a Swiss suburb of Basel. In this building, the architect echoed the curves and arcs of the German factory and museum design. He used the same zinc roofing material, but the façade of the headquarters building is brightly painted stucco. He designed a centrally located "villa" structure against the backdrop of a rectilinear office building. Joined to the large office block by an atrium, the smaller villa structure served as a more intimate space and as a kind of social heart of the headquarters facility. The cafeteria was located there, as were meeting rooms and a reception area.

The German furniture company Vitra commissioned Gehry to design a museum, to house its collection of contemporary chairs, and a factory. The sloping, plaster-and-stucco structure consisted of Baroque arcs, undulating ramps, and gentle spirals that "imply collective movement, responding to the dynamic nature of the manufacturing center."

Colliding volumes

The Vitra projects saw the first appearance of Gehry's signature "colliding volumes." That concept would inform a number of Gehry's subsequent designs, including four of his best-known built structures: the Walt Disney Concert Hall in Los Angeles, the Guggenheim Bilbao in Bilbao, Spain, the Nationale-Nederlanden Building in Prague, Czech Republic, and the Experience Music Project in Seattle, Washington—none of which would have been possible without computer design technology.

Gehry began working on his dazzling Walt Disney Concert Hall in 1987. It was his biggest hometown project, and he conceived it as part of a cultural hub in the center of downtown Los Angeles. He reportedly envisioned the building's main foyer as a natural "living room" for LA. The structure, under construction at this writing and scheduled for completion sometime in 2003, occupies a full city block at the intersection of First Street and Grand Avenue in the historic Bunker Hill section of Los Angeles, right next door to the Music Center of Los Angeles. The Hall will serve as the new home of the Los Angeles Philharmonic orchestra.

Years of design revisions saw Gehry's original stone exterior evolve into a waving, swooping mass of curved stainless steel panels, designed to echo the interior curves of the concert spaces. The entrance to the main lobby features towering glass panels at the top of a sweeping, grand stairway that ascends from an oval courtyard area. An urban park intended for public gatherings will surround the building. When the project is completed, the park will feature public gardens, ornamental landscaping, walkways, benches, and shade trees.

Gehry's original design defined the building's central auditorium as a cluster of intimate boxes opening onto the performance area. Working with acousticians Yasuhisa Toyota and Minoru Nagata, Gehry modified that concept considerably. The 2,265-seat concert hall would eventually assume the form of a convex box, bowed in the middle, and raised on either end, which has been called a "vineyard" configuration. This space, with its ceiling and walls of Douglas fir paneling, is tailored to convey orchestral sound as effectively as possible.

The audience is positioned around the orchestra platform for both acoustic and aesthetic reasons. A 36-foot (11m) rear window and skylights open the hall

Gehry's hometown project, the Walt Disney Concert Hall, was conceived as part of a cultural hub in the center of downtown Los Angeles. Gehry's original stone exterior evolved into a waving, swooping mass of curved stainless steel panels, designed to echo the interior curves of the concert spaces. The Hall, currently under construction, will eventually serve as the new home of the LA Philharmonic orchestra.

Gehry's best-known work is the celebrated Guggenheim Museum in Bilbao, Spain. Conceived after but completed before the Disney Concert Hall, the Guggenheim Bilbao's curvaceous, free-form, sculptural style became a Gehry signature.

Gehry's Guggenheim Bilbao is located at a bend in the Nervión River and serves as a kind of gateway to the city's business and historic districts. Sensitive to the surroundings in which it would stand, Gehry incorporated water-filled pools and even the river itself into the museum's design.

to light during the day. And an enormous pipe organ, which Gehry designed with organ designer Manuel Rosales, rises up within the seating blocks at the rear of the stage. The plan also calls for two outdoor amphitheaters: one, a theater for children's programming that will seat up to 300 kids or 200 adults; the other, a second performing space that will accommodate an audience of 120.

Sensual origami

Easily Gehry's best-known work is the celebrated Guggenheim Museum in Bilbao, Spain. Reportedly, Gehry's plan for the museum began as quick sketches on hotel stationery, drawn after his visit to the proposed construction site in 1991. Other sketches followed, which were developed into physical models. The models were eventually digitized for further manipulation with computers. Gehry's firm utilized CATIA to design and engineer the museum; it is thought to be their first use of the software on a large-scale project. The results have been likened to "a gigged ship," "a castle of ice," and "sensual, space-making origami." The natives of Bilbao reportedly refer to it as "the artichoke." Conceived after, but completed before the Disney Concert Hall, the Guggenheim Bilbao's curvaceous, free-form, sculptural style became a Gehry signature.

Started in 1991 and completed in 1997, the Guggenheim Bilbao was a collaboration between the New York–based Solomon R. Guggenheim Foundation and the Basque regional government. Bilbao is the fourth largest city in Spain, a gritty industrial port in the Northern Basque region, and a stronghold of the separatist group ETA, which seeks independence from Spain. The museum was part of an economic redevelopment plan, designed to improve the city's image. The Basques took on the cost of the $100 million project, and agreed to pay the operating costs of the new museum; the Guggenheim Foundation runs the facility, with its 257,000 square feet (78,400 square meters) of exhibition space. By all accounts, the project was a win-win for all concerned, and it has succeeded in creating an iconic identity for Bilbao.

Gehry's design departs radically from the traditional white cube of museum architecture. The building's irregular geometries are clad in one-third-inch-thick (8.4mm) titanium panels that seem to flutter around the exterior. Although curving metal exterior cladding has become something of a Gehry hallmark, the Guggenheim Bilbao represents the architect's first use of titanium. The panels were applied using a traditional locked seam, creating a softening pillow-like effect. Gehry chose the metal because of its responsiveness to changing light conditions. Alongside the flowing titanium, limestone and large, slanted expanses of grid-enclosed glass define interior spaces.

Gehry has described the overall design as evoking the image of a ship. Speaking with National Public Radio reporter David D'Arcy in 1997, Gehry talked about the goal of his design:

Artists really want to be in an institution that has presence in the city. With most museums that have been built since the war, architects have been very deferential. They've proceeded in reverence for the art as the object to be displayed, and they created these deferential neutral boxes and spaces, which stood for nothing in the community in the end. If you go to Bilbao ten years from now and you don't know anything about [Guggenheim Director Thomas Krens], Gehry, and the Basques, you'll come in to the town and you'll say, "Man, these people really loved art." And that's what artists need, want, crave—that the palaces for their work be just that and be as important as the courthouse and library and city hall.

As much as Gehry's museum might seem at first to stand out from its surroundings as a discrete sculptural object, it does, in fact demonstrate a clear acknowledgement of the environment in which it exists. Located at a bend in the Nervión River (really an estuary wending in from the Atlantic coast) on a former industrial site, the building stands amid a freight yard stacked with shipping containers, a heavily trafficked bridge, and the water. Indeed, Gehry designed the structure to extend out over the Nervión and to incorporate water-filled pools and the river itself. From this position, the museum serves as a kind of gateway to the city's business and historic districts.

In a 1997 interview with the Newshour's Elizabeth Farnsworth, Gehry talked about the influence of the site's disparate surroundings on his design:

...we're on the river in Bilbao; it's a port that's being the accession—moved closer to the ocean. It's all industrial. It's quite tough industrial-looking, and it's surrounded by these green hills, which is very forgiving and makes the industrial palatable. Artists love Bilbao because of this feeling of toughness and solidity and no frills. It's kind of an essence, and so I had a 19th century city up on the hill, up higher, and I had the river and this huge bridge bisecting the site that I had to reconcile. So it's obvious I made the top part relate in simpler forms, blocky forms, to the 19th century city. On the river I made kind of a boat shape. I'm a sailor, so I use those—I love that kind of imagery, and I absorb the big bridge, which if

Evoking the image of a ship, Gehry's
Guggenheim Bilbao stands on a former
industrial site amid a freight yard stacked
with shipping containers, near a heavily
trafficked bridge, and the water.

Inside, the Guggenheim Bilbao is divided into uniquely configured exhibition spaces of "nonrepetitive geometries" designed to accommodate installations of contemporary art. The galleries lead from a central hall, the summit of which is 55 meters above floor level. The hall acts as a large sundial, producing different shadows and effects throughout the day.

you're standing on the river side of the building and you look up, the traffic looks like it's going into the building, and it's—it's very dynamic, and it kind of fits visions of fantasy cities by [filmmaker] Fritz Lang... [W]here you saw these ramps and moving cars up in the air coming into buildings and stuff, and so I built on that idea.

Inside, the building is divided into uniquely configured exhibition spaces of "nonrepetitive geometries" designed to accommodate installations of contemporary art; one writer described them as "a group of free-flowing volumes that seem to have met in a train crash." But he also included rectilinear galleries for the presentation of easel painting and traditional sculpture. The galleries lead from a central hall, the summit of which is 55 meters above floor level. The hall acts as a large sundial, producing different shadows and effects throughout the day. And a long, low space extends out from the central section, runs along the river and under a freeway bridge, and then emerges on the other side.

Body language

None of Gehry's designs represent a more literal interpretation of his "colliding volumes" than his Nationale-Nederlanden Building, better known by its nickname, "Fred and Ginger." Constructed in 1996 in the Czech Republic, the building was designed in collaboration with Studio Vlado Milunic. The steel, glass, and concrete office building stands on a prominent corner across from a public square and a major bridge, in a riverfront neighborhood in central Prague.

The neighborhood is filled with older, five- and six-story row houses, and Gehry's design takes the colors and forms of the surrounding buildings into account. The principal façade of the seven-story building, which overlooks the riverbank, features staggered windows and undulating, horizontal striations that gradually break into a pattern of undulating cornice lines—a kind of riff on the look of surrounding buildings.

But the aesthetics of Gehry's design veer dramatically from its environment with some unique features—most prominently, the dual corner "dancing" towers from which it gets its nickname. One tower ("Fred" for dancer Fred Astaire) is a solid, precast concrete cylinder, slightly flared at the top and bottom, and crowned with a tangled ball of copper; the other ("Ginger" for, of course, his partner, Ginger Rogers) is a tapering glass tower, pinched at the waist and flared much more dramatically at the bottom, evoking the image of a skirt. At the fifth floor, a small canopy juts out from Ginger's waist toward Fred, suggesting a kind of abstract reference to the arms of the dancing couple.

The locals call it "the **blob** at the bottom of the Space Needle," and Gehry's Experience Music Project is probably one of Gehry's **blobiest** designs. Located in downtown Seattle, the 140,000-square-foot (43,000 square-meters) building comprises a cluster of multicolored, organic forms clad in a variety of materials, including steel, glass, sheet metal, and 21,000 colored shingles.

Fred was formed from precast concrete panels, and blends in with the rest of the structure. Ginger consists of two layers of steel-supported glass. The interior layer is the actual wall of the building; the outer layer acts as a screen for the office spaces underneath. Both towers are supported by columns—one straight pillar in Fred's case, and several curving, sculptural columns in Ginger's—which create a small covered entrance plaza for the glass-enclosed first floor. What has been called the "body language" of the two animated towers prompted the moniker. Ginger, with her vertical steel T-members twisting and curving in two directions, appears to lean into Fred. (The designers at Gehry's firm called the building "the Wave.")

Rock temple

Gehry is said to have based his design for Seattle's museum of pop music, the Experience Music Project (1996–2000), on the shape of a shattered Fender Stratocaster guitar, one of the smashed instruments of the legendary Jimi Hendrix, known for destroying guitars during performances. Gehry reportedly bought several Strats, cut them to pieces, and used them as building blocks during the development of the design. The name of the building derives from Hendrix's band, the Jimi Hendrix Experience, and perhaps from a lyric from one of his songs, which asks, "Are you experienced?" But the locals just call it "the **blob** at the bottom of the Space Needle."

Indeed, the EMP is one of Gehry's **blobiest** designs. The project was funded and championed by Microsoft billionaire Paul Allen, who was a fan of Gehry's horse-head shaped conference center at the DG Bank Building (1995–2001) in Berlin—another **blobby** building, which Gehry once called "the most mystical thing I've ever done; the best shape I've ever made." (Gehry reportedly took a rare turn at designing the DG Building directly on a computer.)

Located in downtown Seattle (the late Mr. Hendrix's hometown), the 140,000-square-foot (43,000 square-meters) building comprises a cluster of multicolored, organic forms clad in a variety of materials. Designed to serve as an "interactive" rock museum, it was constructed of steel, glass, sheet metal, and colored shingles—21,000 of them in 3,000 seven-shingle panels. The outlines of the pieces were generated randomly on a computer, and Gehry employed them to echo the colorful body of an electric guitar. Utilizing epoxy-based colored terrazzo, autobody-finish-coated concrete, interference-colored stainless steel, and cast-glass tiles, he arrived at a multihued structure of mirrored purple, brushed silver, bead-blasted gold stainless steel, and red-and-blue painted aluminum.

The vivid building houses kiosks offering interactive tours of rock history, a treasure trove of rock'n'roll memorabilia—from Bob Dylan's 1949 Martin guitar to Janis Joplin's boa to Paul Allen's vast personal collection of Hendrix memorabilia to 80,000 Hendrix artifacts. An existing monorail sweeps through the building headed for the Seattle Center, which also houses 35,000 feet (10,700 meters) of exhibition space, a restaurant, a bookstore, and offices.

Gehry based his design for Seattle's museum of pop music, the Experience Music Project (1996–2000), on the shape of a shattered Fender Stratocaster guitar, one of the smashed instruments of legendary rocker Jimi Hendrix. Gehry reportedly bought several guitars, cut them to pieces, and used them as building blocks during the development of the design.

chapter 3
new **tools**
of the trade

Information-age
architects and
designers animate
the process

For Frank Gehry and his associates, the computer serves as an adjunct to a more traditional, paper-and-model-based design approach. But for a growing number of architects and designers, the computer has become *the* tool of the trade, both for its ability to boost efficiency and for its extraordinary versatility as an artistic instrument. In fact, many are finding that paper can become a genuine hindrance—literally a physical barrier—to the levels of productivity the market demands. By one estimate, Gehry's decision to switch from limestone to metal cladding on the Disney Concert Hall project required 5,000 new drawings. Clearly, clients who want an architect of Gehry's stature are unlikely to worry about whether he generates his remarkable designs on a Mac or scribbles them with a ballpoint on cocktail napkins. But in a world where changes can generate thousands of documents, dynamic design technologies are fast becoming a competitive differentiator.

Computers aren't exactly new tools in this trade. Architectural practices and industrial design firms have been utilizing computer-aided drafting programs for more than a decade, and that technology is quite mature. However, the unorthodox application of dynamic modeling software and animation applications to architecture and industrial design is a comparatively recent phenomenon. Architects such as Greg Lynn and designers such as Karim Rashid have appropriated software intended for film special effects and computer game development to

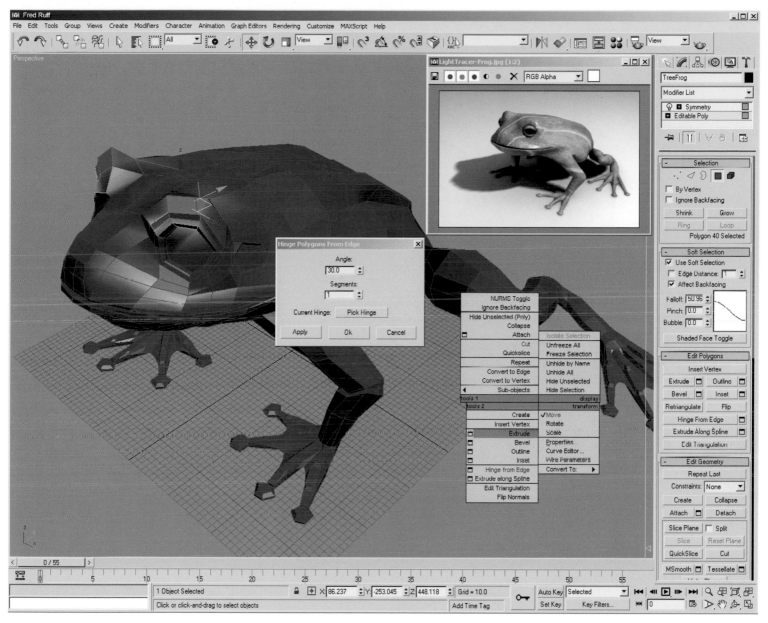

For years, software makers have refined modern animation technologies into sophisticated toolsets for creating computer-generated images (CGI) that are all but indistinguishable from reality. Today, applications like 3ds max, from Discreet, are essential tools of animators, digital artists, and Hollywood special-effects specialists.

render their designs in ways that are simply beyond the capabilities of traditional CAD software. Software applications such as Maya, Softimage, Rhino, formZ, and 3ds max are becoming as commonplace among designers as the venerable AutoCAD.

Karim Rashid wondered about the increasingly central role these kinds of computer programs have begun to play in the creative processes of many designers in his book, *Karim Rashid: I Want to Change the World:*

Are our objects a result of new computer-aided tools of morphing? …I see that we are shaping a world inspired by these highly complex dimensional tools. NURBs, splines, metaballs, and other bioshaping commands are fostering a more relaxed organic condition…I can take any sacred geometry… a cube, a sphere, a cylinder, and collage them together or metaball them into a liquid plastic biomorphic form that I can regulate—softer, globular, or tighter and more defined.

What is perhaps most intriguing about this trend is that Rashid, Lynn, and others are using these technologies, not merely to render and refine their ideas, but to discover new things about them. These programs have become, in a sense, collaborators in the creative process for many

who use them. Lynn has openly acknowledged this increasingly symbiotic relationship between designer and computer. "If it comes down to it," he told *Lingua Franca*'s Alexander Stille in a 1998 interview, "I would have to give the software 51 percent of the credit for the design of my buildings."

CAD/CAM: Essential tools of digital design

The first computer-aided design systems—better known as CAD—began appearing in the 1970s. It is no exaggeration to say that the advent of CAD technologies changed fundamentally the way plans, schematics, models, and blueprints are created in virtually every quarter. These systems allow designers and architects to work fast and to generate incredibly complex designs without producing mountains of paper. Graphics files need not be redrawn for every change in a design. Templates can be applied to standard forms. Files can be forwarded easily to clients via email. And the renderings can allow clients to see images of their projects from virtually any angle.

The CAD software available today is a universe beyond the crude, 2-D drawing applications that seemed so advanced twenty years ago. Those older systems relied on terminals linked to large mainframe

Given the ability of tools like Auto-des-sys's formZ general purpose solid and surface modeler to articulate 3-D spaces and forms, it's hardly surprising that architects and industrial designers are adapting them to their own purposes.

Auto-des-sys bills its popular formZ digital design software, which was used to create the images on this and the next page, as a "3-D synthesizer." This sophisticated modeling tool is widely used by architects, illustrators, industrial designers, computer game developers, and others.

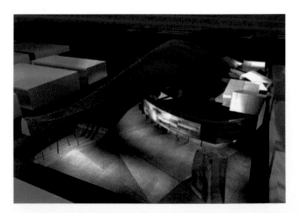

computers and didn't do much more than a paper-based approach. According to Marian Bozdoc, author of *The History of CAD*, the first graphic system was developed in the mid-1950s at the Massachusetts Institute of Technology for the United States Air Force's SAGE (Semi Automatic Ground Environment) air defense system. Built at MIT's Lincoln Laboratory, the system displayed computer-processed radar data and other information on what amounted to a TV screen.

Early CAD programs used simple algorithms to display patterns of lines, at first in two dimensions, and later in 3-D. Dr. Patrick J. Hanratty, known as the Father of CAD/CAM for his pioneering contributions to the field of computer-aided design and manufacturing, developed the first commercial system in 1975.

It was the advent of personal computers in the early 1980s that allowed CAD systems to evolve into practical tools for mainstream designers. By that time, CAD technology had been used for years to design aircraft components and so-called big-iron computing systems. Now, with powerful computing capacity migrating to the desktop, software makers began developing computer-aided design systems that were within the economic reach of architects and industrial designers.

One of the first of these was John Walker, who founded Autodesk in 1982. The northern California-based company's mission was to create a CAD program with a price tag of around $1,000. The company succeeded with the release of Auto-CAD. The venerable application, today a true industry standard, was based on a CAD program written in 1981 by Mike Riddle.

CAD systems today couple high-speed computer workstations or desktop machines with 3-D software and sophisticated graphics tablets for natural drawing input. Generic systems are widely available, as are systems with special features for architectural, electrical, and mechanical design. Design systems may also be highly specialized to accommodate the unique demands of things like computer circuit-board design.

Even more complex programs allow designers to engage in "solid" and "parametric" modeling, both of which involve the generation of virtual objects within the computing environment that have real-world characteristics. In solid modeling, objects can be sectioned (sliced down the middle) to reveal their internal structures. In parametric modeling, objects can be programmed to have specific and

limited relationships with each other; doors, for example, may be assigned to appear only in walls, but never in floors.

Perhaps one of the most important developments in the evolution of CAD technology is its pairing with computer-aided manufacturing software (CAM). The integration of CAD and CAM allows designers to input their electronic plans directly to the machines that will assemble them, eliminating yet another gap between designer and end product.

NURBs and **blobby** objects
The earliest 3-D modeling systems relied on equations that defined points on a surface, which generated polygons that could be connected to depict surfaces in a kind of wire mesh configuration. These polygonal meshes were useful for rendering mechanical

forms, but fell short when it came to rendering organic shapes. Humans and animals rendered with this technology tended to look like badly whittled marionettes. Additionally, generating curved surfaces using polygons requires lots of computing power (it takes a lot of little angles to create a curve), making the process both time-consuming and tiresome.

The advent of so-called spline-based modelers made it possible to render much smoother and more varied forms. Outside the digital world, a spline is a flat, pliable strip of wood or metal bent into various shapes, and used to draw complex curves on paper. In computer graphics, the term refers to a smooth arch that runs through a series of user-controlled points, which may be called knots, nodes, anchors, or control-points—in other words, a curved line. Other points not on the spline may be employed to control the shape and sharpness of the curve. Spline-based modelers use nets of curved lines to define the surface dimensions of objects. As users of these tools pull and manipulate the net, the computer recalculates the overall surface shape to keep it smooth.

There are several types of splines: Bezier splines, cardinal splines, cubic splines, NURBs, Catmull-Rom splines, and Hermite splines, to name a few. A Bezier spline is a curve generated with a mathematical formula developed in the 1960s by French auto designer Pierre Bézier. The most commonly used Bezier curves today are fully defined by just four points: two endpoints and two control points that do not lie on the curve itself, but describe a shape that determines the path of the curve. Bezier splines or b-splines are used to construct "patches," which in turn form complex surfaces that are markedly smoother than their polygon equivalents.

NURB modelers represent a further refinement of this technology. NURB stands for Non-Uniform Rational Bezier spline, which is a type of very flexible b-spline. NURB curves can represent any shape from a straight line to a circle or ellipse very precisely and with very little data. They can also be used for guiding animation paths, for approximating data, and for controlling the shapes of 3-D surfaces. NURB-based modeling systems are known for their ability to control the smooth-

ness of a curve. And they are considered much easier to work with because users can manipulate the surfaces of their models by moving virtually any point on the form.

The digital objects called "metaballs" provide designers with an even more sophisticated technique for realistically rendering truly organic forms. While polygonal-, spline-, and NURB-based technologies essentially render the surface contours of various forms, metaballs—also called meta-elements, **blobby** objects, or simply **blobs**— read as "solid" spheres and ellipsoids. Where polygonal systems create forms based on mathematical relationships among explicit points, metaballs rely on implicit representations, where the surface of the object is defined as the zero contour of a function of two or three variables.

In other words, a metaball is a three-dimensional variable-density field radiating from a given center point. Metaball fields can be altered and influenced by other metaballs in myriad ways. A metaball's virtual "weight" can be changed, which causes its shape to change. The fields of overlapping metaballs can be encouraged to intermingle (the

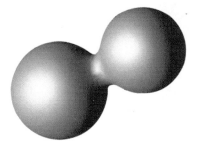

The digital objects called "metaballs" provide designers with a more sophisticated technique for realistically rendering truly organic forms. A metaball is a three-dimensional variable-density field radiating from a given center point. A metaball's virtual "weight" can be changed, which causes its shape to change. The fields of overlapping metaballs can be encouraged to intermingle, blending the forms to produce composite surfaces and complex shapes.

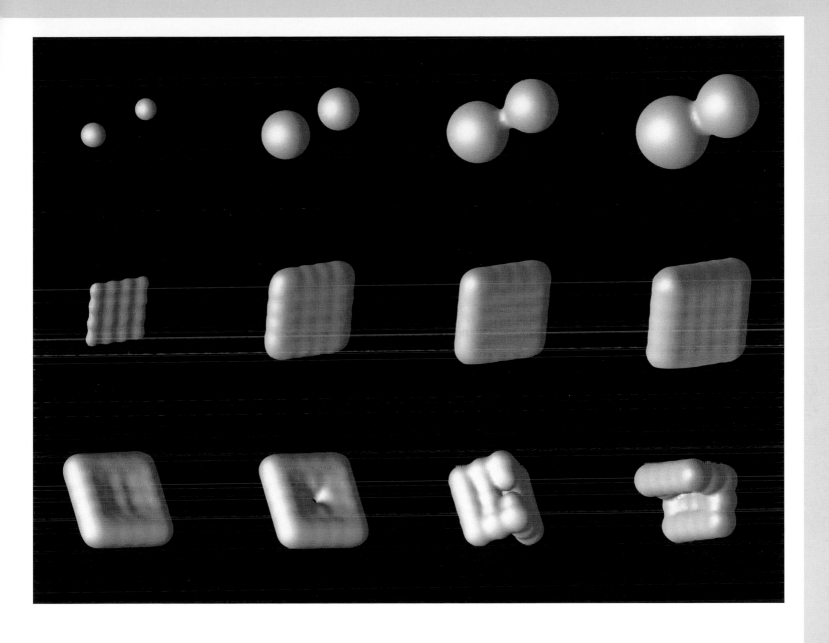

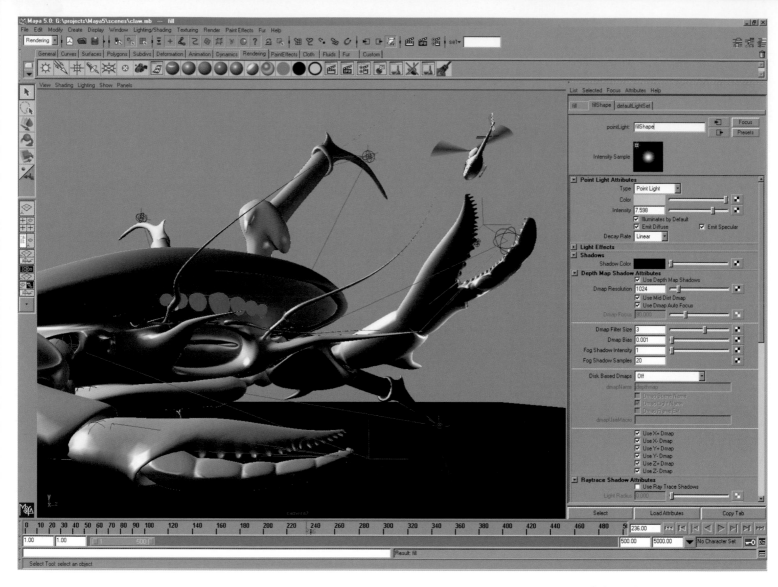

Software design programs, such as Alias/Wavefront's Maya, have become essential tools of animators, digital artists, and Hollywood special-effects specialists.

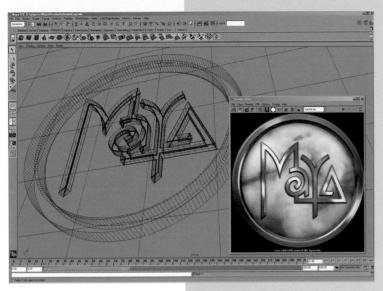

Alias|Wavefront received an Acadamy Award in 2002 for its Maya 3D animation, dynamics, modeling, and rendering production tool. Maya was used in two of that year's Oscar winners; *Lord of the Rings: The Two Towers*, winner of the best visual effects, and the *ChubbChubbs!*, winner of the best animated short.

process is called "fusion"), blending the forms to produce composite surfaces and complex shapes. Manipulating metaballs, designers—primarily animators—are able to render a limitless range of organic forms, from water to people.

Animating forces

In 2000, architect Greg Lynn talked with *New York Times* reporter Eric Taub about the essential advantages of designing with computers. "Without a computer, every point on a structure has to be calculated with reference to everything else," Lynn said. "But by using a PC, I can create complex curves that don't have radii or centers. Since the entire form is tied into itself through a complex mathematical equation, I can easily push and pull the shape and have the equation automatically recalculate the new relationships within that form. If I tried to do that by hand, a day's work would take a couple of years—literally."

Lynn is famous for reaching beyond traditional CAD/CAM tools to work with the dynamic computer modeling systems employed in movie animation and special effects to "evolve" his designs. Lynn is cred-

ited with coining the term "**blob** architecture" back in 1995, which he later told *New York Times* columnist William Safire refers to the acronym for Binary Large OBject. A **BLOB** is a large, single block of data stored in a database. Typically, **BLOBs** are multimedia objects, such as pictures, video, and sound. They're called "large" because a **BLOB** may have an enormous storage capacity. Some database administrators say that the name also suggests, albeit inadvertently, what a gooey pain these files are to deal with.

Confusing matters just a bit, "**blob**" (lower case) is also a computer graphics term that refers to a malleable virtual object used in animation—the metaball previously described. Whatever its etymology, Reed Kroloff, editor of *Architecture* magazine, eventually shortened Lynn's expression to "**blobitecture**."

Writing in his book, *Animate Form*, Lynn touches on the implications of employing animation software to architecture:

The challenge for contemporary architectural theory and design is [to] try to understand the appearance of these tools in a more sophisticated

way than as simply a new set of shapes. Issues of force, motion and time, which have perennially eluded architectural description due to their "vague essence," can now be experimented with by supplanting the traditional tools of exactitude and stasis with tools of gradients, flexible envelopes, temporal flows and forces…. Because of the present lack of experience and precedent with issues of motion and force in architecture, these issues might best be raised from within the technological regimes of the tools rather than from within architectural history…

In other words, the evolving capabilities of the tools themselves are challenging longstanding notions about architecture and design—or at least they are making such a challenge unavoidable.

Software vendors have been refining these technologies for years into powerful programs for creating computer-generated images (CGI) that are all but indistinguishable from reality. Today, these applications are essential tools of animators, digital artists, and Hollywood special effects specialists.

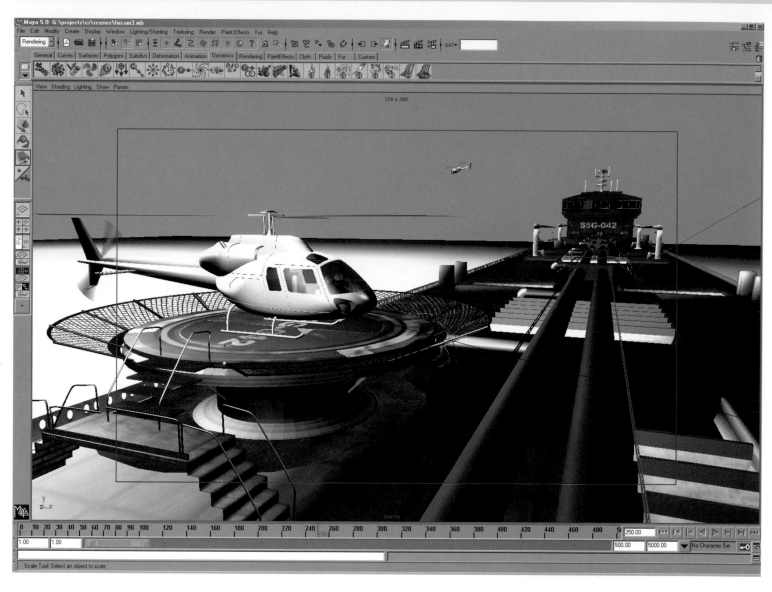

Animation software presented **blob** architects and designers with more than simply a new set of shapes. These powerful tools allowed them to add the elements of force, motion, and time to their designs.

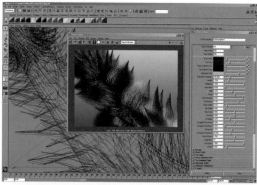

The evolving capabilities of the computer animation tools themselves are challenging longstanding notions about architecture and industrial design.

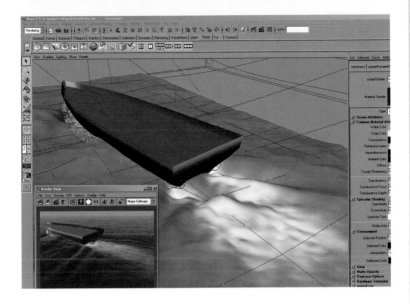

One of the early pioneers in this field was Daniel Langlois, a Canadian filmmaker who founded a company called SoftImage in 1986. Dissatisfied with existing animation technology, which was complicated and technical, used mainly by engineers, Langlois set out to create a 3-D animation system "for and by artists." The notion of approaching software from the perspective of creators was a genuinely revolutionary at the time.

In 1987, Langlois and engineers Richard Mercille and Laurent Lauzon began work on an animation program that would be accessible to non-techies, while exploiting the power of a newly emerging generation of high-end computer workstations. The application they created would become the company's flagship offering: Softimage/3D.

In its initial incarnation (launched in 1988 as Creative Environment), the program combined for the first time all the processes of 3-D image development, including modeling, animation, and rendering. As the product evolved, it would become the first commercial package to support inverse kinematics, a technique that allows elements of an animated object to be linked so that its movements are realistic relative the other elements—say, an upper and lower arm, or eyebrows on a face. The famous "actor module" earned Daniel Langlois a Scientific and Engineering Award from the Academy of Motion Pictures Arts and Sciences in 1998. It would eventually include the first production-speed ray tracer. Ray tracing is a rendering method that simulates shadows and light reflections and refractions.

The company's official corporate history explains it this way:

The system offered a complete integration of traditional tools, using 3-D (modeling, animation, rendering), which were often separate processes in other products. SoftImage was the first to offer a product where artists had complete access to tools without having to follow a path or a sequence of operations. This type of workflow was different from the rest of the market and launched SoftImage as a company very quickly.

It's probably not an exaggeration to say, as the company often does, that SoftImage/3D "generated a new breed of visual effects artists and animators." Corporate hyperbole notwithstanding, the product's influence was sweeping, and it dominated its market for more than a decade. Industrial Light and Magic, Digital Domain, Sega, Nintendo, and Sony have used SoftImage tools. They have been used in hundreds of major feature films including *Titanic*, *The Matrix*, *Men in Black*, *Star Wars: Episode I—The Phantom Menace*, *Gladiator*, and *Harry Potter*, among many others, as well as a host of computer games (Super Mario 64, Tekken, Virtual Fighter, Wave Race, and NBA Live).

Microsoft acquired the Montreal-based operation in 1994. Microsoft later sold SoftImage to Avid Technologies, well known for its film and video editing systems. SoftImage 3D's star faded a bit in the blazing glow of another popular 3-D animation product, Alias/Wavefront's Maya, but the company's latest offering, the SoftImage XSI 3D non-linear production environment, reclaimed some of its lost luster in the early 2000s.

Maya, one of the most popular and widely used 3-D animation tools for feature films, is the progeny of two innovative graphics software companies, merged in 1995. Alias/Wavefront was formed when Silicon Graphics, Inc., bought Alias Research of Toronto and Wavefront Technologies of Santa Barbara and put together the best features of all their products.

Alias Research was founded in 1983 by Stephen Bingham, Nigel McGrath, Susan McKenna, and David Springer, who, much like SoftImage's Langlois, set out to create an easy-to-use software package to produce realistic 3-D video animation for the advertising industry and

Today's sophisticated software tools
make it possible to render hyperreal
images for movie special effects and
computer games. The three images
shown here were created with Discreet's
3ds max.

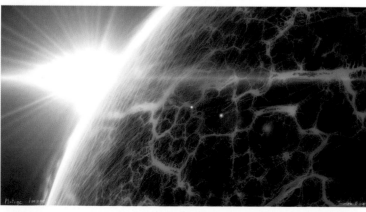

post-production houses. The company describes Springer, who was teaching computer programming for designers at Sheridan College when he met McGrath, as a "rare combination of artist and computer programmer." Springer had been working independently on software that resembled ideas on which McKenna and Bingham had also been working.

Working out of a renovated elevator shaft in a building in Toronto, the four founders developed Alias/1. Based on "natural" or "cardinal" splines, the tool produced much smoother and more realistic surfaces than polygonal lines.

Before the company was acquired and merged with Wavefront, Alias developed a number of popular products, including Alias Studio and Alias Power Animator. Alias Studio is a product design software package still widely used for industrial and vehicle design; Power Animator (basically the same program with additional animation functions) is still used by a few companies in the entertainment industry.

In 1989, Alias helped Industrial Light and Magic create the pseudopod creature for *The Abyss*. Alias 2.4.2 was used to model the creature because it was b-spline-based, instead of polygonal, which gave the filmmakers the smooth, waterlike effect they were after. *The Abyss* is hailed by the film industry as one of the most technologically advanced and difficult motion pictures ever filmed. In fact, it won an Oscar for Best Visual Effects. The Alias tool also helped the makers of *Terminator 2: Judgment Day* construct their liquid metal man, whose onscreen antics garnered another special-effects Oscar.

Wavefront Technologies was founded in 1984 by Mark Sylvester, Larry Barels, and Bill Kovacs. The three founders formed the company to produce computer graphics for television commercials and movies. Because no off-the-shelf software was available for this purpose, they adapted their business plan and set out to develop and market their own computer graphics software.

During its first year of operation, Wavefront used its Preview product to create opening graphics for Showtime, BRAVO, and the National Geographic Explorer. Universal Studios later used Preview on the TV series *Knight Rider*. Wavefront's product lines included Kinemation, a 3-D character animation system for creating synthetic actors with natural motion and muscle behavior, and Dynamation, a powerful 3-D animation tool for interactively creating and modifying realistic, natural images of dynamic events.

It took the combined companies nearly three years to produce their joint flagship product, but the marketplace seemed to feel that it was worth the wait. In 1998, Alias|Wavefront introduced its Maya line, and the tools quickly ascended to the top of the heap. Celebrated for their ability to render rigid objects, soft bodies, fluids, cloth, hair, and realistic flesh tones, the Maya tools utilizes the MEL (Maya Embedded Language) scripting language to define sequences.

In 2000, Maya was used to create the top four selling titles for the PlayStation 2 console: Electronic Arts' Madden NFL 2001; SSX: Snowboard Supercross (EA); Tekken Tag Tournament (Namco); and NHL 2001 (EA). That same year, all three Oscar nominees for Best Visual Effects used Alias|Wavefront software: *The Matrix*, *Stuart Little*, and *Star Wars: Episode I—The Phantom Menace*. (*The Matrix* won.) In 2001, Maya software was used in the production of a 23-digital-person cast for the animated film *Final Fantasy*. Maya was also the main 3-D modeling and animation software used in the production of *The Lord of the Rings: Fellowship of the Ring*, released in 2001. The film included 570 digital effects shots, which included, in the words of the company, "everything from elaborate and other worldly 3-D environments and complex bluescreen and miniature composites, to fantastical 3-D creatures, huge armies of CG soldiers and peasants, and photorealistic digital doubles of nine of the principal actors in the film." The filmmakers snatched up the software when it was first released in 1998, and Maya served as the primary 3-D application for the production, according to Jon Labrie, chief technical officer at Weta Ltd., the New Zealand–based production company behind the films.

These software lines are just two examples from a burgeoning array of increasingly sophisticated computer-aided design applications that are fast becoming commonplace, as familiar in so-called paperless practices as T-squares and compasses were to a previous generation. For the cutting-edge architects and designers who are utilizing these kinds tools in unorthodox explorations, they offer more than pencils and paper ever could. They represent a kind of doorway into uncharted territories.

The increasingly symbiotic relationship between digital technologies and designers can be seen in an almost loving acknowledgement on the website for Greg Lynn's architectural practice, Greg Lynn FORM. The site declares: "The office views the incorporation of state-of-the-art hardware and software... as a set of tools to investigate architectural performance within the framework of theories based on performance parameters that are only now being theorized in architecture..."

chapter 4

a **blob** by any other name

Greg Lynn creates a manifesto for a new architectonic philosophy

"Waveform" architects, as they are defined by author/architect Charles Jencks, reject the Newtonian idea that matter is a static, passive recipient of forces. "We now understand that matter is much more dynamic and alive than we thought," he told Adam Davidson in a 1999 *Metropolis* interview. "When the Romantics looked at nature, they saw truths that always remained true. When complexity science looks at nature, it sees forces—tectonic plates, for example—that are active and self-organizing and produce interesting results that are different from simple formal results."

Jencks believes that waveform architecture will become "one of the four or five dominant architectures in the next four or five years." And he has called Greg Lynn "the great waveform theorist in the United States."

Architect, teacher, and writer Greg Lynn is certainly **blob** architecture's leading theorist. His radical use of high-end computers and sophisticated animation software has allowed him to push well beyond the limits of traditional forms into a world of extremely plastic and flexible structures. His work during the 1990s and early 2000s with "hypersurface" or waveform architecture put him at the forefront of digital design. *New York Times* architecture critic Herbert Muschamp has called Lynn's work "a genuine mutation, a natural response to the displacement of bricks and mortar by virtual space."

Lynn's architectural firm, Greg Lynn FORM, was established in 1994 in Hoboken, New Jersey, and then relocated in 1998 to Venice, California, to "take advantage of the knowledge and technology

Greg Lynn's conceptual "Embryological House" is the quintessential—if virtual—**blobitectural** structure. It grew out of his interest during the late 1990s in developing a mid-market, single-family dwelling that could be customized easily for virtually any setting. What he developed was a structure defined by a soft, flexible surface of curves, rather than a fixed set of rigid points; what Lynn calls "voluptuous aesthetics of undulating surfaces."

resources in both the manufacturing and entertainment industries of Southern California," according to the firm's website. FORM is a "paperless" studio in which designs are conceived, created, and refined directly on the computer. "With these programs," Lynn has written, "we've shifted to thinking of space as the sheltered enclosures of a flexible handkerchief."

What distinguishes Lynn from a host of other architects working with computers today is his application of animation effects during the design process. The *Times*' Muschamp described Lynn's work with **blobs** in virtual space this way:

Conventional (so-called orthogonal) buildings are typically rendered by plans and elevations, two kinds of two-dimensional drawing. **Blobs**, on the other hand, are rendered as

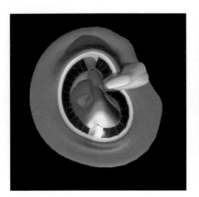
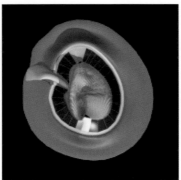
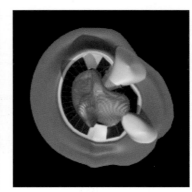
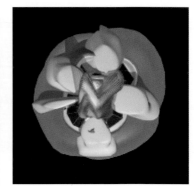

During Lynn's design phase, vectored forces are applied to **blobs** in the virtual design space of the computer. The architect sets the forces, and the software generates a series of spaces that Lynn calls "gastrulated rooms," after the biological process by which an embryo folds onto itself to create a stomach, or gaster.

three-dimensional computer models, like those we see for [car bodies] or molecular structures. By collapsing plan and elevation into a single three-dimensional form, the computer model encourages architects to break out of orthogonal, right-angled space. Instead, they can manipulate all dimensions at once. Space becomes as plastic as a hunk of Silly Putty. It can be pinched, rotated, kneaded, stretched, cut into sections, shattered or left to ooze. The computer model displays the impact of each manipulation on the whole.

The very idea of animation in architecture, of forms that can be "pinched, rotated, kneaded, stretched, or left to ooze"—of buildings as hunks of Silly Putty—seems at first antithetical to such a fundamentally stable and static art. Lynn clarified his thinking on this apparent contradiction in the introduction to his book, *Animate Form*:

In its manifold implications, animation touches on many of architecture's most deeply embedded assumptions about its structure. What makes animation so problematic for architects is that they have

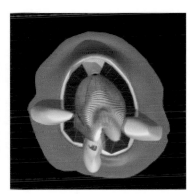

maintained an ethics of statics in their discipline. Because of its dedication to permanence, architecture is one of the last modes of thought based on the inert. More than even its traditional role of providing shelter, architects are expected to provide culture with stasis. This desire for timelessness is intimately linked with interests in formal purity and autonomy. Challenging these assumptions by introducing architecture to models of organization that are not inert will not threaten the essence of the discipline, but will advance it….

In Lynn's paradigm, animation is not motion. Motion is about movement, while animation is about "the evolution of a form and its shaping forces; it suggests animalism, animism, growth, actuation, vitality and virtuality."

This notion of design "evolution" lies at the heart of Lynn's approach and his pursuit of what he calls "dynamically conceived architecture." For him, the technology isn't merely a sophisticated rendering tool, but a participant of sorts in the design process. Yet, Lynn doesn't simply launch **blobs** against each other, hoping that a building might spring from the virtual impact. The relationship between this artist and the tools of his trade is an unconventional one, which Lynn explains this way:

[T]he computer might be considered as a pet. Like a pet, the computer has already been domesticated and pedigreed, yet it does not behave with human intelligence. Just as a pet introduces an element of wildness to our domestic habits that must be controlled and disciplined, the computer brings both a degree of discipline and unanticipated behavior to the design process. By negotiating the degree of discipline and wildness, one can cultivate an intuition into the behavior of computer-aided design systems and the mathematics behind them.

The firm's website fairly trumpets FORM's embrace of digital design technology: "[FORM] views… state-of-the-art hardware and software… as a set of tools to investigate architectural performance within the framework of theories based on performance parameters that are only now being theorized in architecture."

A particularly biomorphic example of Lynn's approach can be seen in an early project: his counterproposal to the Cabrini Green Urban Development competition. Initially conceived as a submission to a 1993 housing design competition in Chicago, Lynn expanded his plans and offered an urban zoning counterproposal "to try to envision a somewhat more radical solution to the problems posed by an utterly failed housing project like Cabrini."

For this design, Lynn and his associates used a combination of computers and plain old pencil and paper. The firm's website describes the process:

After the initial analysis of the site, which took place on paper, we input the site into the computer. The hyperbars were developed using both our hands on paper, to arrive at a convincing way of morphing the housing screed, for example, but also using some images on the computer, and bending them in Photoshop to see how they might reconfigure on the site. The hand-drawn linear hyperbars were then modeled on the computer, and laid into the site, where we were able to bend them within the virtual city, in response to the site conditions. Throughout this process the computer was used as a tool to work in an almost physical way with the models, by bending them, and also provided constant access to the condition of the moving section.

As their organizational model, they selected, not merely a **blob**, but a zooid, an organism produced asexually by budding or fission. Created in the virtual space of the computer, the zooid models would react to site conditions, entered by the designers, first budding in single file, and then responding with forking and branching, what Lynn called the "bifurcating zipper." These "deformations" were a direct response to the demands of the site.

In the final iteration of the project, at what the firm calls "a local level of detail," the zooids would morph in yet another way, evolving an aggregate condition "within which the individuals specialize in function, creating feeding organs, circulatory systems, genitalia, etc." In other words, at this local level, the **blobs** would begin to evolve what might be seen as architectural detail.

Clearly, there's a lot of theory here, but this isn't a matter of sizzle versus steak. Lynn and his team are working at the bleeding edge. By thoroughly integrating the computer into their design process, they have begun to use technology as a tool of investigation as well as expression, as a means of both generating questions and answering them dynamically in animated virtual space. In a few short years they

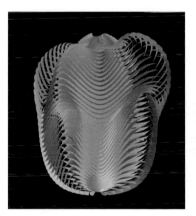 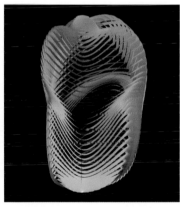 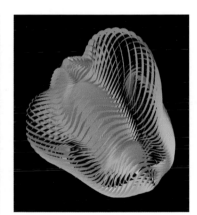 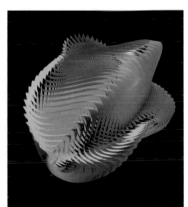

Using his animate approach and
Alias|Wavefront's Maya animation soft-
ware, Lynn defined his Embryological
House as a soft, flexible surface of
curves, rather than as a fixed set of rigid
points.

The lower level of an Embryological House is set into the ground, about halfway down, creating what Lynn sees as a kind of nest. A berm of earth slopes from the lower level to the upper level of the house to meet the front and back entries, making the house appear to be buried in the ground.

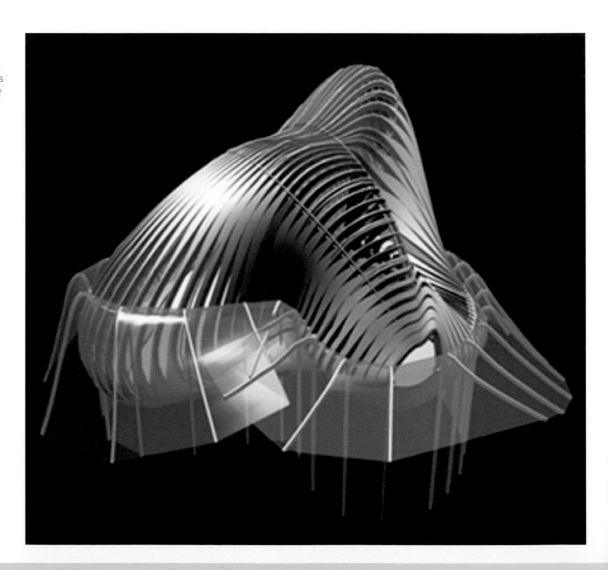

have produced a range of designs that challenge traditional ideas about architecture.

Although many of these experiments with software-driven design have, to date, remained unrealizable in the real world, their impact on architecture has been very real. Lynn's projects, publications, teachings, and writings continue to influence architects and the relationship between advanced technology and human creativity.

Mutations and monsters

Lynn's Embryological House is perhaps the quintessential **blobitectural** structure. In the late 1990s he began developing a concept for a mid-market, single-family dwelling that could be customized easily for virtually any setting. Using his animate approach and Alias|Wavefront's Maya animation software, he defined the structure as a soft, flexible surface of curves, rather than a fixed set of rigid points. The firm's literature describes the concept as "a strategy for the invention of domestic space that engages contemporary issues of brand identity and variation, customization and continuity, flexible manufacturing and assembly, and most important an unapologetic investment in the contemporary beauty and voluptuous aesthetics of undulating surfaces rendered in vividly iridescent and opalescent colors."

That breathless and somewhat hyperbolic language notwithstanding, Lynn's goal here was fairly grounded. Like so many new American houses, the Embryological House would use factory manufactured components assembled on site. But unlike the traditional kit-of-parts approach, these biomorphic structures would not be customized with the addition or subtraction of distinct parts. Instead, Lynn wanted to create a customizable structure that supported "free variation."

"I wanted to take a more biological approach," Lynn explained to *ArtByte* magazine's Mark Dery in a 2000 interview, "where there would be no discreet components. They'd all be in the same morphospace—the same form-space—so that a change in any component would inflect every other component within the system…"

During the design phase, vectored forces would be applied to **blobs** in the virtual design space of the computer; the designer would set the forces, and the software would generate a series of spaces Lynn calls "gastrulated rooms," after the biological process by which an embryo folds onto itself to create a stomach, or gaster. The final structure would be defined as a soft, flexible surface of curves, rather than as a fixed set of rigid points.

"The trick is to set up a design program that would control changes," Lynn told *ArtByte*. "You do the working drawings for what I call the 'seed' of the house, and then the computer generates all the mutations. You never really see the norm; it's all monsters. That's why it's called an Embryological House. You can have young ones, egglike ones that haven't been mutated much, but when these things get adult—in other words, after they've been designed and customized for their context, the client, the whims of the architect, whatever—they mutate into full-blown monsters."

Lynn's penchant for the biological metaphor is particularly apt for this structure, which has a double "skin." Lynn has described the form as an integral shell and frame—Lynn calls it a "monocoque shell"—which ties its lighter and thinner structural components together. The interior is enclosed in a surface composed of over 2,048 panels, all of which are unique in their shape and size. The panels are networked so that a change in any one of them ripples through the building, keeping them always connected, and yet variable. "The variations to this surface are virtually endless," Lynn explains, "yet in each variation there are always a constant number of panels with a consistent relationship to their neighboring panels."

Lynn conceived the building's fenestration system (its windows) as a series of shredded and louvered openings that "respected the soft geometry of the curved envelopes." These "shreds" would give the walls the translucent and filigreed look of a screen. "I wanted to avoid punching windows," Lynn has said, "so the skin has very fine shreds in it; the wall can go from something like punched windows to something like a glass wall, depending on how far apart you have these shreds."

The curved chips of this envelope would be made of wood, polymers, and steel, all of which would be fabricated with robotic computer controlled milling and high pressure water jet cutting machinery, according to Lynn.

Lynn protects this shredded inner surface with a second skin made up of a system of strips that wrap the house and shade the internal layer. These strips are composed of stainless steel and photovoltaic cells, and may be oriented with the angle of the sun in mind to maximize and minimize solar exposure. Lynn has said that the effect is "like being in a jungle. The way the light enters the house—through fronds, and through the arbor of the shading system—make it very aqueous."

The doorway to the Embryological House is a sphincterlike aperture that irises open and closed through the use of counterweights. The interior is divided into upper and lower levels, defining two kinds of living space, which are accessed via moveable ramps or stairways. The lower level is very flat, open, and uncustomized, ready for quick modifications. The upper level is upholstered, carpeted, and veneered, like the interior of an automobile. Appliances and consumer electronics are embedded, and furniture and storage can "inflect, bulge, and gastrulate" from the floors. The floor finishes include cork, artificial leather, wood, MDF, Maderon, stainless steel, rubber, carpet, fabric, ceramics, gel padding, and plastic.

The lower level of the house is set into the ground, about halfway down, creating what Lynn sees as a kind of "nest," about which he waxed poetic in an interview:

A sea of mounds planted with alternating strips of decorative grasses surrounds each house. Nestled within these wave mounds, an undulating berm of earth receives the house. The berm slopes from the lower level to the upper level of the house in order to meet the front and back entries. The house appears to be buried in the ground from some orientations while appearing to float above it from others. Wherever the exterior form of the house is indented, a corresponding garden pod is formed, off which a formal garden flows. These microclimate pods, with their corresponding formal gardens, are ringed by a perimeter of drift gardens that feather into the wave landscape of grasses.

In 2000, Lynn and a team of UCLA students created an exhibit for the Venice Biennale's Seventh International Architecture Exhibition called "The Embryological House." They developed complex, **bloblike** struc-

Lynn conceived the fenestration system (the windows) in his Embryological House as a series of shredded and louvered openings that "respected the soft geometry of the curved envelopes." These fine "shreds" would give the walls the translucent and filigreed look of a screen.

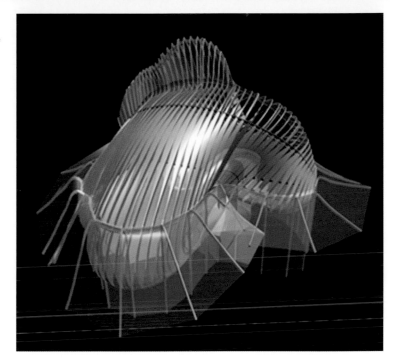

tures into a single-family dwelling using the approach just described. The designs were used to create scale models in wood and plastic, which were displayed along with the computer renderings at the exhibit. To date, these are the only such structures to emerge from the computers virtual design space.

An experiment in contextualism
Lynn utilized the animate approach in 1994 to create a design for the Welsh National Opera House on the Inner Harbor of Cardiff Bay in South Wales. The building site was adjacent to the Oval Basin, an old lock at the heart of the Cardiff Bay area, which had been filled in during the 1960s to stabilize the walls. The old lock was to be restored, and the design brief called for a new building with a symmetrical horseshoe Opera Hall and a strong connection to the historic site. The project, Lynn wrote

at the time, "mandates a new concept for waterfront urban space that is nonetheless continuous with the history of the site and Cardiff's waterfront."

To Lynn, this juxtaposition of objectives made the project an "experiment in the development of new concepts and architectural techniques for contextualism." The task as he saw it was to develop a structure that could be understood as "absolutely continuous with its context while having a distinctly new identity."

Lynn conceived the Opera House as an "urban threshold between land and sea." He drew on the pattern of the graving docks, which connected the land to the water, and integrated his design with a new public reservoir space that would flow under and through the site from the restored Oval Basin. The waterfront's history of boat building and repair

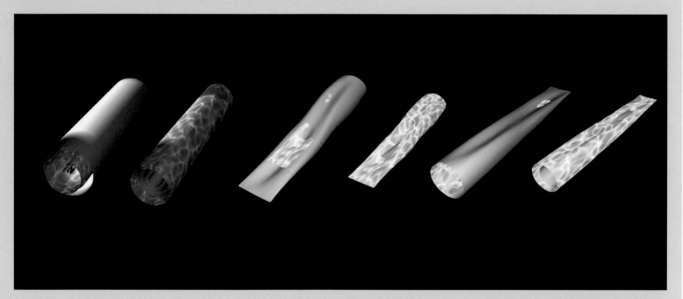

For 1994's Yokohama International Port Terminal competition, Lynn set out to create a design that would enhance as well as manage the flow of pedestrians and cargo to and from a busy Japanese seaport. Lynn stretched his animated **blobs** into tube forms, which would evolve into long, sushilike rolls that, when combined, would open and flatten at the ends to become surfaces.

suggested that the edge adjacent to the old lock should be a key feature of the project. "Our tactic was to exploit the rusting technological husks of the ship-building industry, such as the Oval Basin, as the chrysalis for the symmetrical proliferation of a new urban structure," Lynn wrote.

And he used the very shape of the basin itself as the basic **blobs** of his design. Ovals were repeated, stretched, turned, and aligned in virtual space, resulting in a cluster of ovoid spaces oriented around the edge of the basin, which were further modified as the design evolved. These basic ovals would eventually mutate into facetted polygons, structured by a series of parallel, transverse ribs tied together along ridge beams and keel-like transfer beams—a design analogous to a ship's hull.

The ovoid spaces would be supported by a series of concrete wall fins, which would allow sections to "float" above the sunken area of the site on the lock side, creating open spaces by the water for continuous public use. And the supports would be sheathed in a lightweight tensile membrane that would allow for a diffused light that would change throughout the day. The firm's literature describes the effect this way:

The translucency of the building would transform at dusk when the skin would become a glowing surface during the evening and night. The inter-space that emerges between the support walls, the hull-like volumes, the lightweight tensile skin and the reservoir below the site becomes the dynamic and multiply programmed space of a new civic institution and an urban space and image that does not mimic the historic context in its relationship to the Oval Basin and Oval Piazza.

The final design included stages, foyers, shops, dressing rooms, rehearsal rooms—all set at one half level above grade—recording studios, a three-story public space connected to a partially underground parking garage, and the Oval Piazza. The performance and rehearsal spaces would be isolated from external vibration and noise because of their independent structures. And a series of ramps would slope down to the Oval basin from various levels of the building

Fluid streams of movement
For 1994's Yokohama International Port Terminal competition, Lynn set out to create a design that would enhance as well as manage the flow of pedestrians and cargo to and from a busy Japanese seaport. Originally constructed in 1894, the Osanbashi Pier is considered Japan's marine gateway. In 1988, the city of Yokohama began construction to replace the aging pier and later called for designs for a new passenger terminal.

The eight-acre site is located between two parks, including Yamashita Park, the oldest harbor park in Japan, and a sports stadium. The city wanted a terminal that would serve as both a gateway to Yokohama and an extension of the surrounding public spaces. The design also called for a mix of civic facilities in a single building.

Lynn wanted to look beyond the traditional notion of a threshold or doorway, to provide instead a "continuous sequence rather than an abrupt transition between the land and sea by occupying the threshold and stretching the duration of arrival along the entire length of the pier."

To that end, Lynn stretched his animated **blobs** into tube forms, which would evolve into long, sushi-like rolls that would open and flatten at the ends to become surfaces. The terminal tube would begin as a surface, an open plaza, at the city side of the site, and then roll up to form the tube and, at the ocean side,

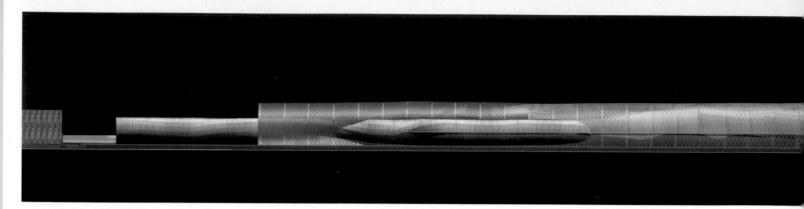

Lynn's Yokahama Port Terminal comprised a series of tubes threaded through one another, based on the docking patterns of the ships, and mingling interiors and exteriors. The terminal tube would begin as a surface, an open plaza at the city side of the site, and then roll up to form the tube at the ocean side. Another tube would begin as a surface at the ocean edge, and then curl into a tube leading toward the city, terminating in a large parking garage.

a departures and arrivals terminal. The so-called citizen's tube would begin as a surface at the ocean edge, making a public park space at the water ferry stop, and then curl into a tube leading toward the city, terminating in a large parking garage with an empty center through which visitors entered the terminal hall. The public tube would terminate into a suspended moss garden that would push through the top of the building to become a roof garden.

Also, the tubes would be threaded through one another based on the docking patterns of the ships, linking the spaces. As these spaces passed though one another, their interiors and exteriors would intermingle. The interior spaces would include a departure lounge, a cafeteria, shops, and a conference center; the open spaces would provide observation decks, access to the moss garden, and a parking deck.

"Because these sequences are passing through one another," Lynn writes in *Animate Form*, "the passengers arriving to the city of Yokohama are experiencing the citi-

zens' garden. Similarly the citizens share in the experience of transportation. The project intermingles these two passages, so that one is always participating in aspects of both simultaneously."

Lynn's design called for the tubes to be sheathed in different materials. The terminal tube would be clad in lead-coated stainless steel to weather the extreme sea climate of the site. The citizen's passage, with its garden and water landscape, would be enclosed in a lightweight tent structure that filters natural light and allows for a more translucent connection to the city and sky. A lightweight steel lattice with cable trusses would support the various roof members.

"The project captures the streams and flows of passengers and citizens in a dynamic mixture," Lynn writes. "It is not a vertical threshold that occurs abruptly but a horizontal duration of space and time between city and garden."

A portrait of movement
In 1995 Lynn and company submitted a design for the Port Authority

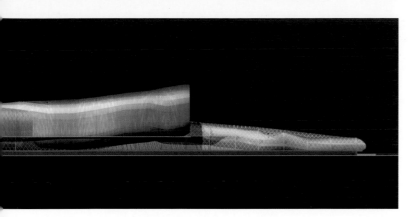

Gateway competition. The challenge here was to create a protective roof and a lighting scheme for the underside of a series of bus ramps leading into New York's Port Authority Bus Terminal.

Utilizing his animation approach, Lynn worked out his design in virtual space, applying forces to his **blobs** to simulate the movement and flow of pedestrians, cars, and buses across the site. The software allowed him to simulate the differing speeds and intensities of traffic moving along Ninth Avenue, 42nd Street, and 43rd Street, as well as four elevated bus ramps emerging from below the Hudson River. "These various forces of movement," Lynn writes, "established a gradient field of attraction across the site."

To "discover" the shape of this invisible field of attraction, Lynn introduced particles into his virtual design space that would change position and shape according to the influence of the motion forces. The density of the particles would increase as they were attracted by these forces. The massing particles would gel into cloud forms, providing

The Yokahama Port Terminal's ovoid spaces would be supported by a series of concrete wall fins. The supports would be sheathed in a lightweight tensile membrane that would allow for a diffused light that would change throughout the day.

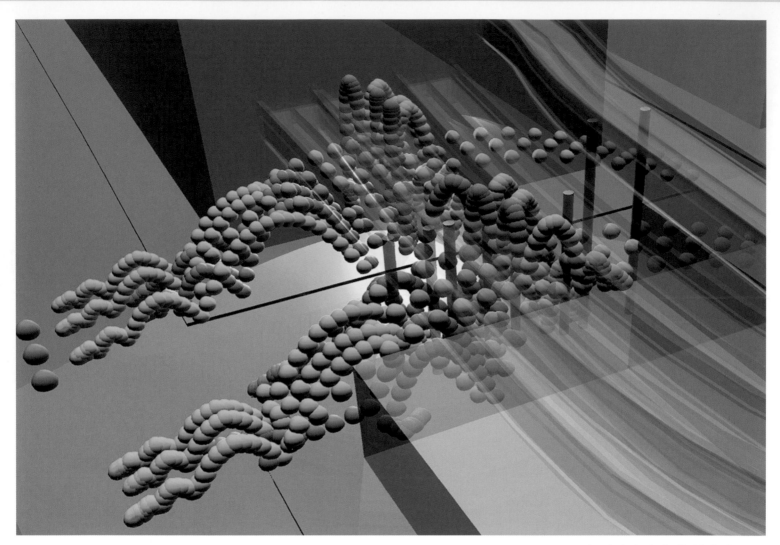

Lynn's design for the Port Authority Gateway Competition was based in part on "particle studies" to understand the movement and flow of pedestrians, cars, and buses across the site. He used an animation "sweep" technique to create a portrait of the cycles of movement over a period of time.

Lynn with the visual representation he was looking for—essentially providing a map of the flow of pedestrian, auto, and bus traffic across the site.

This "particle study" yielded a kind of portrait of cycles of movement over time. Using an animation "sweep" technique, Lynn captured a sequence of positions through a phase of this motion. As Lynn explains in *Animate Form*, "Particles released both from the west façade of the bus terminal and on the street level of Ninth Avenue are the source of these sweeps. Because these particles have elasticity and density, and because they move in a space with gravitational force, the paths take the shape of gravity-resistant arches."

These sweeps lead to the development of a secondary structure of tubular frames that would ultimately link the ramps, existing buildings,

and the Port Authority Bus Terminal. The finished design included 11 tensile surfaces stretched across these tubes; lightweight fabrics (which Lynn, ever reliant on the biological metaphor, calls "membranes") would serve as a roof, but also as a projection surface. As the firm explains it, the project would combine a display surface where information regarding the transportation systems of the city would be projected, with a canopy that supports informal and temporary programs requiring shelter from the rain and sun. On this tent structure videos, text, and images would be projected at various scales at various times of the day providing information to visitors, commuters, and residents.

This tentlike roof would also provide a sheltered multiuse space for vendors and pedestrians. At night, the covering could simply be

illuminated from below to provide a "glowing canopy."

A new media canvas
Lynn seemed to expand on his projection-surface canopy idea to a much grander level with his design for the Eyebeam Atelier Museum of Art and Technology in New York. Here, Lynn further blurred the boundaries between technology and architecture with a building concept that literally combined the two. Eyebeam Atelier is a SoHo-based, not for-profit new-media arts organization. In 1998, the group began planning a $40 million, 90,000-square-foot (27,400 square meters), Manhattan-based museum devoted solely to digital arts. The museum would be a "new facility dedicated to the dialogue between art and technology." The new Eyebeam building would be designed to provide production and exhibition opportuni-

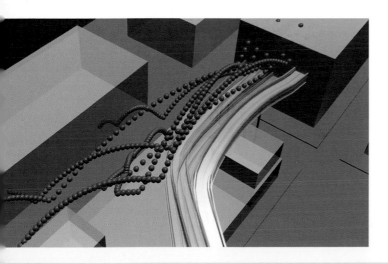

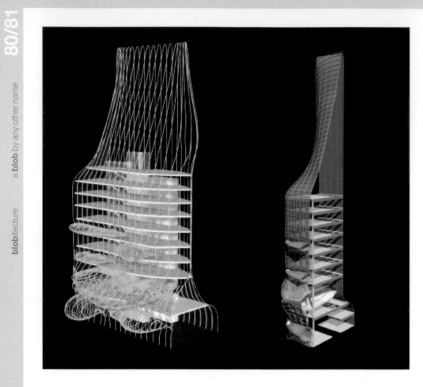

At the base of the Eyebeam Atelier Museum, Lynn's "media skin" would bunch into intricate folds, creating pockets of space that would act as portals for pedestrians to interact with the culture and programming of the Museum.

With his design of the Eyebeam Atelier Museum of Art and Technology in New York, Lynn sought to create "a monumental membrane between the physical and electronic world." The multistory museum for the SoHo-based new-media arts organization would be sheathed in a "media canvas" that would support projections of images and messages on a grand scale.

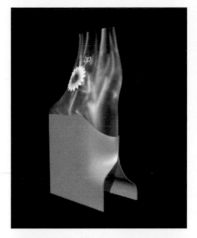 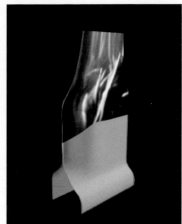

 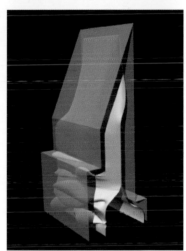

ties for artists exploring new media in video, film, and moving image art, DVD production, installation, 2-D/3-D digital imaging, "net" art, and sound and performance art forms.

Lynn and company saw the museum project as an opportunity to build an "icon and symbol, not only for the state of art and technology, but also to create a monumental membrane between the physical and electronic world." The proposed structure would be wrapped in a "new media canvas," and the interior would swirl with twisting corridors that pierced the building façade.

The multi-story structure would rise tall in the New York skyline, like a beveled monolith sheathed in its media canvas, "enabling the projection of constantly changing array of messages and images, establishing a dialogue with the public and the environment of the metropolis."

At the base of the building, this media skin would bunch into intricate folds, creating pockets of space that would act as portals for pedestrians to interact with the culture and programming of the Museum. *Metropolis* magazine's Marc Kristal described these folds as "goiterlike extrusions and intrusions in the building's skin." According to Lynn's firm, the interior of these spaces would have "a degree of neutral flexibility punctuated by fixed portals through which images from the Museum mingle with the imagery of the city. These portals are the nodes of both physical and visual circulation through the museum."

Lynn considered his version of the Eyebeam museum to be a kind of permanent art installation. The firm's literature calls the project "the first not-for-profit application of a moving image on a building surface," and points to the inevitable economics of this point of view: "It is now economically and technically viable to understand the surface of a building as being more valuable than

Lynn partnered with Michael McInturf and Douglas Garofalo to design the Korean Presbyterian Church of New York. The Sunnyside, Queens, church was converted from a derelict 1930s factory building. The final design is an integrated combination of the original structure and the new components, of stucco and sheet metal cladding.

its interior, given particular locations in the city. The tower is a medium in itself, another channel for broadcast."

A hybrid in real space

Probably Lynn's best-known built project as of this writing involved the alteration of an older structure. Lynn designed the Korean Presbyterian Church of New York, completed in 1999, in partnership with architects Michael McInturf and Douglas Garofalo. Located in Sunnyside, Queens, the church was converted from a derelict 1930s factory building, which had been vacant since its previous occupant, the Naarden Perfume Company closed down in 1986. Architect Irving Fenichel designed the two-story, 88,000-square-foot (26,800 square meters) art deco building in 1931 for the Knickerbocker Ice Company, which housed its laundry business there. The Knickerbocker Laundry had been gone since about 1970, but the company cleaned uniforms for the Yankees baseball team, which made the building something of a local landmark

The church's largely Korean immigrant and first-generation-American congregation gave the designers a relatively free hand, and a $10 million budget. After years of holding services in other recycled buildings, they were open to unconventional design ideas. In fact, they had a few of their own. "The clients wanted the traits of a church," Lynn recalled in an interview, "such as a focus on the altar, a central axis, and backlighting, but they didn't want a cathedral or cruciform plan."

The church, which sits amid used car lots and shopping malls off Northern Boulevard, would need to function as a social and educational center for the Korean community. In addition to the sanctuary itself, the final design would include 80 classrooms for Sunday school and other purposes, a wedding chapel for 600, four multipurpose assembly spaces, a library and exhibition center, a rehearsal space for a 200-member choir, offices, and outside parking for 350 cars.

The design began, of course, as **blob** forms in virtual space. In fact,

the designers, who practiced in different cities at the time, collaborated strictly in virtual space via linked computers from the project's inception through the development and construction document phases. (Lynn was still in Hoboken, Garofalo was based in Chicago, and McInturf's home base was Cincinnati.) Working this way, the designers combined **blob** elements with the conventional box form of the existing structure to create a hybrid design, what the *Times'* Muschamp called a "para-building—an addition that radically transforms what came before."

"We wanted the addition to seem like it was responding to the existing building without seeming like an addition and without swallowing it up into a new whole," Lynn said.

The designers sought to retain "the industrial vocabulary of the existing building and transform its interior spaces and exterior massing into a new kind of religious building." To this end, the exterior of the old factory building was renovated to something approaching its original

The most striking feature of the Korean
Presbyterian Church of New York is its
massive, open sanctuary space. The
2,500-seat sanctuary comprises an
asymmetrical space, with angled banks
of seating and angular overlapping inside
wall planes. The sanctuary ceiling is
composed of a series of sharply angled
rib forms that, should they collapse, will
"nest" against each other.

state; its windows were replaced with aluminum-frame storefront windows and the precast cladding was repaired. The original building was designed with an oversized façade meant to get the attention of commuters passing by on the train; the designers kept the old facade intact, but painted black.

The final design is an integrated combination of the original structure and the new components, of stucco and sheet metal cladding. Three intersecting "tubes" or corridors weave vertically through the structure, providing traffic circulation and containing entrances, hallways, stairs, and elevators. An exterior staircase, partly enclosed in a tunnel-like structure, shields arriving congregants from the largely industrial neighborhood that surrounds the church—yet provides a view of the Manhattan skyline as they leave. Three bridges and wide flights of steps connect the parking lot to two glazed entrances next to a new three-story translucent fiberglass facade.

The most striking feature of the building is its massive, open sanctuary space. The *Times'* Muschamp called the space "the most impressive interior to be built in New York in many years." The 2,500-seat sanctuary (seating capacity roughly equal to St. Patrick's Cathedral) comprises an asymmetrical space, with angled banks of seating and angular overlapping inside wall planes. The sanctuary ceiling is composed of a series of sharply angled rib forms that, should they collapse, will "nest" against each other.

The sanctuary sits on what was the factory roof and is enclosed by a monumental long-span ceiling. Structurally, it was designed as an independent shell within the rooftop shed, with its own support columns threading through the factory to separate foundations—the only way the old roof would support the congregation.

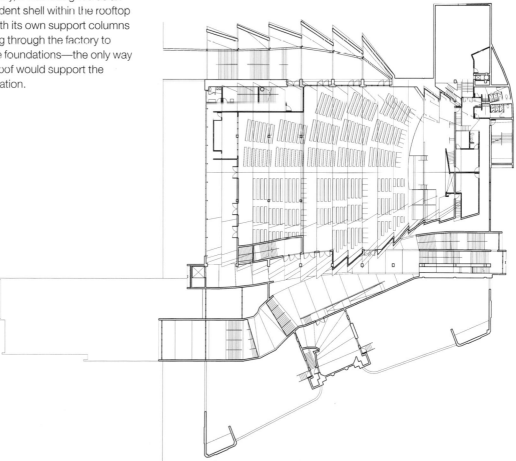

biological thinking

Architect Norman Foster's spherical London City Hall has been likened to an egg, a bubble, and even a giant testicle. The striking ten-story glass-and-steel structure stands on the south bank of the Thames River. Its unusual shape was intended to minimize the surface area exposed to direct sunlight and improve energy efficiency.

Designed in 1996 to serve as a *pied-a-terre* for a Manhattan couple, the Ost-Kuttner Apartment displays the smoothly merging interior surfaces that are characteristic of many of Kolatan and Mac Donald's digitally generated designs.

The digitally evolved structures of **blob** architecture are "less built than born," wrote Mark Dery in *ID* magazine. And yet the **blobists** weren't the only contemporary architects begetting a brood of curvy and sinuous buildings. A similar architectural biomorphism may be seen in the works of a host of designers not strictly identified as **blobmeisters**. Particularly during the 1990s and early 2000s, fluid forms characteristic of **blobitecture** manifested in the designs of several cutting-edge architects.

Breeding hybrid identities
The amorphous, computer-generated "chimerical hybrids" of Sulan Kolatan and William Mac Donald represent an attempt to liberate architecture from its traditional building blocks. The highly biomorphic forms of many of their digitally mutated designs go every bit as far as Greg Lynn in challenging architectural convention. Biomorphism informs Kolatan/Mac Donald's Resi-Rise concept for a high-rise building with customizable "pod" apartments; it can be seen in the

smoothly merging interior surfaces of their Ost-Kuttner Apartment in Manhattan.

The architects elaborate on their approach to creating such "hybrid identities" on the Kolatan/Mac Donald Studio website:

One of the emerging spatial paradigms is that of the network as a system of interrelations between dissipative processes and aggregative structures that shape new spatial patterns and protocols.... Our work focuses in particular on the network model's capacity to facilitate cross-categorical and cross-scalar couplings whereby the initial systems/morphologies are not merely interconnected, but form new hybrid identities. What differentiates this new generation of chimerical hybrids from previous mechanistic ones is the act of transformation. These new systems are not determined and cannot be understood through a logical extension of the initial parts alone. They are hybrid, but nonetheless seamlessly and inextricably continuous....

Kolatan and Mac Donald develop their designs through a twofold procedure that employs "co-citation mapping" and the "chimera." The chimera, which is a reference to a mythological lion-goat-snake monster, is a symbol of the hybrid forms they create:

The chimerical differs in crucial ways from other forms of hybrid systems such as collage, montage, or the prosthetic. While the latter are also systems in which the diverse parts operate together, these parts never lose their individual identities. We have two primary interests in the chimerical. One has to do with its seeming capability as a concept to help define existing phenomena of fairly complex hybridity in which categorically different systems somehow operate as a single identity. The other is based on the assumption that the ways in which chimera are constituted and operate hold clues to a transformatively aggregative model of construction/production. That is to say, an aggregation which becomes more than the sum of its parts, and there-

In the construction of Raybould House, Kolatan and Mac Donald employed a system of concrete panels coated with a flexible mixture of aluminized polyurethane. In this building (shown opposite), concrete took on the role of both structure and surface.

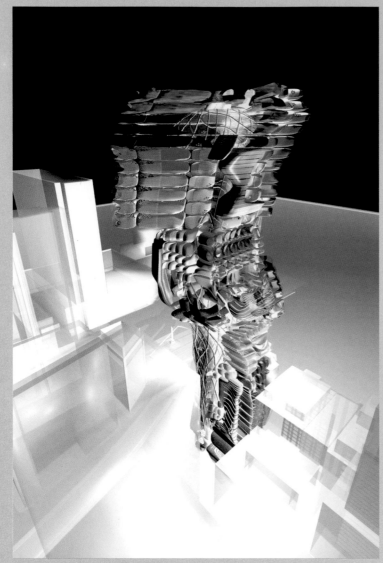

The computer-generated "chimerical hybrids" of Sulan Kolatan and William J. Mac Donald represent an attempt to liberate architecture from its traditional building blocks. That idea can be seen in Resi-Rise, their concept for a high-rise building with customizable "pod" apartments.

fore is not reducible to its constituent parts. Thus, the chimerical has the potential to be both an analytical and methodological tool.

Co-citation mapping is a computer technique, a form of electronic indexing and information retrieval. The architects describe it this way:

As an index, it works according to a similar principle as any keyword-based library search, listing all work related to the same keyword and thus revealing non-apparent conceptual connections across categories such as humanities and science, for example. Interestingly, the next level of organization is constructed as a map, a geographic description of relational knowledge. They have no absolute axis. Instead their spatial organization is based on continually becoming hierarchies which are contingent upon frequency of citation and thus subject to change over time.

Combining the two produced Raybould House, a project that called for a new house situated on a partly wooded plot of land and connected to an existing "saltbox" house. A barn and a swimming pool were also already extant on the property.

Kolatan and Mac Donald call their solution a "chimera-like hybrid between the logic of the existing architecture and that of the surrounding landscape." Composed of a system of concrete panels, clad with a flexible mixture of aluminium-ized polyurethane, the house reflects the surrounding landscape in its curving lines and irregular contours.

They describe their highly conceptual Housings as "chimerical houses for mass customization." In this project, the two architects drew on co-citation mapping and the chimera model to conceive a long-term project that focuses on experimental designs for mass-customized, prefabricated housing.

The idea of drawing design variations from a kind of digital gene pool has a lot in common with Greg Lynn's basic notions about **blob** architecture. Information for this "genetic pool" would be generated from the specifications of a representative three-bedroom-two-and-a-half bath colonial house plan, stored on the computer. The system would identify these specs as a "base," and establish a range of "object-products" as "targets." Blending the base digitally with different targets would produce variations in the design, spawning a variety of "chimerical houses." Kolatan and Mac Donald write:

"Housings" sets out to explore the question of serial and organic compositeness in architectural design on three parallel tracks. One, in relation to digital processes with their capacity for variable iterations, organic transformation, and cross-referencing. Two, in regards to

Kolatan and Mac Donald view Raybould House as a chimaera-like hybrid between the logic of the existing architecture and that of the surrounding landscape. The lines and contours of the site and the irregular outlines of the structure inform one another.

issues of viability: can a hybrid outperform existing normative types in a particular social, cultural, economic, ecological, geological, and climatic life-context? And three, vis-à-vis an emerging generation of composite materials and digital production technologies.

Tinkering with toroids

Preston Scott Cohen likes to challenge our preconceptions about the nature of order in architecture. He is known for combining advanced digital modeling techniques with his personal fascination for 17th century descriptive geometry.

Cohen uses computer technology extensively to integrate seemingly contradictory architectural notions. **Blobs** and biomorphic structures, for example, are not generally considered amenable to mathematical quantification, and are thus widely viewed as anti-modernist. And yet, by using digital design tools to describe irregular forms mathematically, Cohen manages to mingle, if not precisely blend, modernist ideas about form and function with the sensuous, organic curves that animate his designs. In Cohen's work, we see familiar forms distorted by the computer to create complex and original spaces.

Cohen's Torus House is a good example of his fusion. On one level, it is a design for communal living, a house in which a group of single residents come together to share living expenses, provide social support, ease the environmental impact of their consumption and energy use, and create special-interest networks. On another level, it represents Cohen's ongoing experimentation with space and community.

Definitions of a torus may be found in four academic disciplines: In the field of anatomy, it refers to a bulging or rounded projection or swelling; in botany, it's the receptacle of a flower; in architecture, it refers specifically to a large rounded molding that wraps the base of a classical column; and in mathematics, it is a surface with the shape of a doughnut. All of these definitions are suggestive of what Cohen is up to with Torus House, but his notions about "toroidal architecture" lean toward the last one. In a torus, the outside surface traverses the center, reversing the familiar relation between inside and outside. In Torus House, the lines from the ceiling to the walls and floor appear to be folds in a single surface rather than orthogonal intersections among separate planes.

Like Cohen's earlier, single-family home, Turtle House, this design is based on circular spaces, which are seen in both the private and common rooms of the house. Circular rooms, the architect says, are the most energy efficient and "the most comforting to us, psychologically."

The arrangement of the interior spaces of this design grew out of an organic model, which Cohen explains this way:

In nature, the most important parts of an organism are always located at its center. It only follows logically that when designing a house, the most important rooms should be in the middle. In Turtle House, designed for a nuclear family, the bedrooms were in the middle; but in Torus House, a communal cooperative housing unit, the common room is in the center.

For Housings, Kolatan and Mac Donald drew from a kind of digital gene pool, generating designs from the specifications of a representative three-bedroom-two-and-a-half bath colonial house plan, stored on the computer, which was blended digitally with different "targets" to produce variations in the design.

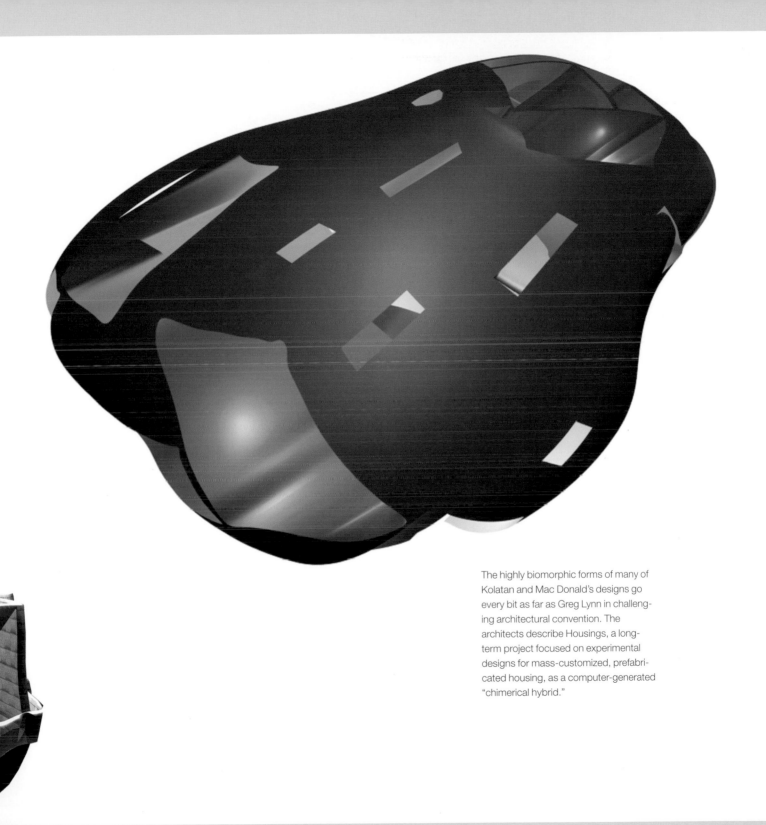

The highly biomorphic forms of many of
Kolatan and Mac Donald's designs go
every bit as far as Greg Lynn in challenging architectural convention. The
architects describe Housings, a long-
term project focused on experimental
designs for mass-customized, prefabricated housing, as a computer-generated
"chimerical hybrid."

Torus House provides bedrooms for eight individuals with private closet space and one toilet for every two residents. Because they are arranged around the outer wall, the bathrooms and showers have windows; the bedrooms and central common room do not, but receive natural light from large skylights. The core of Torus House contains a stair that allows residents to pass from a parking platform below the house directly to the roof without entering the building.

One of Cohen's stated goals with this design is to facilitate interactions among residents. Consequently, each occupant shares a shower with one person, but a bathroom with a different person. And doors must be left open if air is to circulate within each room.

Hatching a great steel-and-glass egg

Many of the designs of Pritzker Prize winner Norman Foster, principal at Great Britain's Foster and Partners architectural practice, evince an organic aesthetic. His City Hall in London, for example, has been likened to an egg, a bubble, and even a giant testicle. Writing in the *Telegraph*, Giles Worsley observed that the spherical building, with it's zigzagging lines of windows, "is strangely reminiscent of the comic-book hero Judge Dredd's helmet." Deyan Sudjic, writing in the *Observer*, called it a "a wacky object sitting in the middle of a flat field" and a "gray **blob**."

Completed in 2000, the building stands on the south bank of the Thames River. The ten-story, glass-

Norman Foster's London City Hall features a large, spiraling ramp that winds to the roof, offering changing views of London. The interior space is filled with offices, committee rooms, public facilities, and a large assembly debating chamber with a 250-seat viewing gallery, open to the public.

The British Museum's Great Court is the largest enclosed public space in Europe. Foster's design features a glazed canopy that spans the irregular gap between the Reading Room dome and the restored 19th-century facades. The lattice steel shell forms both the primary structure and framing for the glass, which is designed to reduce solar gain.

and-steel structure features a large, spiraling ramp (reminiscent of Preston Scott Cohen's torus) that winds to the roof, offering changing views of London. Inside, the space is filled with offices, an assembly debating chamber, committee rooms, and public facilities. The large, open debating chamber is a key feature. Located on the top floor, the space includes a 250-seat viewing gallery, open to the public. The gallery offers views over the river to the Tower of London through a triangulated glass facade.

The building's egg shape was intended, at least in part, to minimize the surface area exposed to direct sunlight. According to the firm, the shape of the building "is derived from a geometrically modified sphere, a form which contains the greatest volume with the least surface area." Foster and Partners used computers to calculate exactly how the sun would strike the structure on every day of the year. Using those data, he adapted factors such as the shapes of the building's walls and the opacity of the window glass to maximize energy efficiency. Foster

expected these design considerations to reduce the amount of energy the building consumed to approximately one-quarter of the energy used by conventional buildings. The building's actual energy consumption has reportedly not met that estimate.

The computer played a significant role in the building's construction, as well. Digital design specifications in CAD/CAM software guided computer-controlled steel-cutting mills, which turned out components of the structure, like puzzle pieces, that were then assembled on-site.

In a 2000 interview with Hugh Pearman of the London *Times*, Foster said of his design, "It's not whimsy. It's rooted in an incredible intellectual rigor, planning rigor, structural rigor, environmental rigor.... It takes that quest for a better working environment one notch further."

Scheduled for completion in 2004, Foster's equally organic Sage Gatehead music center is a 2,000-seat facility located on the south bank of the Tyne River in Tyne and Wear, England. The building will

Foster's design of the Expo Station on the Changi Airport Line in Singapore includes two dramatic overlapping roof structures. One is a 40-meter-diameter stainless steel disc covering the ticket hall; the other is a 130-meter-long ellipse clad in titanium, which shelters the passenger concourse.

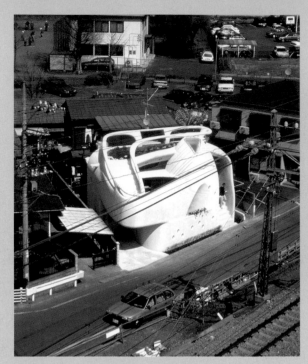

Constructed in 1993, Kathryn Findlay and
Eisaku Ushida's white, sculptural Truss
Wall House stands in stark contrast to its
surroundings on a tiny site, squeezed by
a rail track in Tokyo.

house three auditoriums, each
conceived as a separate enclosure,
and the Regional Music School. The
entire complex will be sheltered
beneath a broad, enveloping roof
"shrink-wrapped," as the firm puts it,
around the buildings beneath and
extending over the concourse. The
distinctly biomorphic curves of the
silver roof structure will echo the
great arch of the nearby Tyne Bridge.
Cafés, bars, shops, an information
center, and the box office will occupy
the concourse. The space beneath
the concourse will house the music
school.

Unifying British and
Japanese aesthetics
The designs of the husband-and-
wife architectural team of Kathryn
Findlay and Eisaku Ushida explore
the psychoanalytical and "psycho-
geographical" components of
architecture but seen within a
context of scientific research into
form. Findlay is a Scottish architect
trained to revere buildings that are
responsive to their surroundings;
Ushida is Japanese, educated in a
tradition that values an artful formal-
ism in buildings designed to exist as
discrete sculptural objects. Together,
they are developing new ways of
thinking about architecture that
incorporate both of these points of
view. In a way, they are unifying what
might be thought of as British and
Japanese aesthetics.

"They're part of a tradition of
waveform architecture," architectural historian Charles Jencks said in
a 1999 interview. "They are involved
in the translation and transformation
of chaos theory, complexity theory,
fractal theory, and a whole host of
new theories of science into a theory
of design."

Greg Lynn has described their
work as "calculus-based form, architecture with smooth topological

surfaces," and he sees their fluid
designs as very similar to his own.
Indeed, the architects have said that
the movements of the human body
inspire the organic shapes of their
buildings.

That similarity is particularly
apparent in Ushida and Findlay's
Truss Wall House, constructed in
1993. The white, sculptural form of
this two-story private dwelling, their
second home design, stands in
stark contrast to its surroundings on
a tiny site, squeezed by a rail track in
Tokyo. In a speech she gave in 2001,
Findlay described the design as a
"fluid kind of space" based on the
sequence "in, through, up and out."

The client for this project was the
owner of a building company that
had developed a patented system
for casting concrete in fluid forms.
Ushida Findlay used computer-
aided design software to design an
inner truss frame of compound
curves, and used the client's system
to create that frame in reinforced
concrete.

A double-wall envelope encloses
the building's interior, with insulation
and air cavities between. This inner
layer serves as a kind of second
skin, which Ushida Findlay have
called a "thermo-dynamic organ,"
that stabilizes the environment
inside. According to the architects,
the flowing interior is "intended to
create space, as a fluid continuity of
sensuousness and physical imagery
which is disseminated with a
person's movement through that
space." These spaces "emulate the
flow of pliable viscera which is
packed into a vessel" to become a
"frozen fluidity." This organic
aesthetic is echoed in the "soft"
hand-brushed mortar surfaces of
the inner walls.

Six steps lead from the street to a
living and dining area on the upper
floor, where a circular seating area

For Truss Wall House, Ushida and Findlay used computer-aided design software to create an inner truss frame of compound curves, and a system for casting concrete in fluid forms developed by the owner of the house to create that frame in reinforced concrete.

Zaha Hadid emphasized the "urban character" of the environment in her design for the National Centre for the Contemporary Arts of Rome. Scheduled to open in 2005, the art center will stand on the site of an old army barracks between the Tiber River and Via Guido Reni.

with a built-in sofa sits under a dome-shaped ceiling. Glass doors open onto a small, tiled courtyard, from which stairs lead to a small roof garden. More stairs lead down to bedrooms on the lower floor and a kitchen with built-in shelves.

"In a remarkably eclectic city, the forms, the materials, and the site plans of their houses bear no resemblance to those of other structures," Adam Davidson wrote in *Metropolis*. "Among the clean modernist lines and planes of their neighbors, Ushida Findlay houses twist and bulge bizarrely. In a country where every architect hopes to create an ideal form, Findlay and Ushida prefer to blur the distinctions between their creations and the natural landscape."

Laying urban carpets

London-based architect Zaha Hadid has made a career of pushing the envelope and challenging popular convention. She has been called the "queen of architectural avant-garde," and she often bases her designs on architectural paintings and drawings that she creates during the production phase of her process. But many of Hadid's architectural projects are so complex that they are simply impossible to design on the drafting board alone. Consequently, she also relies on animation software in her pursuit of innovative uses of light, space, and shadow. Hadid's design portfolio includes large-scale urban studies and built work. She also designs interiors and furniture. "[Hadid's] designs... were flowing and flamboyant decades before Frank Gehry's Guggenheim Museum became the icon of Bilbao in Spain," *Time*'s Rod Usher observed.

Hadid is known for her futuristic architectural language and spatial approach to design. Her big idea—one of them, anyway—is a concept she has dubbed the "urban carpet," which she defines as a continuous surface between the street outside and the walls inside. This concept informs her National Centre for Contemporary Arts in Rome, Italy, about which she has written:

At times, it affiliates with the ground to become new ground, yet also ascends and coalesces to become massivity where needed. The entire building has an urban character, prefiguring upon a directional route connecting the River to Via Guido Reni, the center encompasses both movement patterns extant and desired, contained within and outside.

Scheduled to open in 2005, the art center will stand on the site of an old army barracks between the Tiber River and Via Guido Reni, where the building "absorbs the landscape structures, dynamizes them and gives them back to the urban environment"—in a way, intensifying the surrounding space. Hadid's design maintains a kind of respect for context that acknowledges the art center's urban environment, by retaining what she calls an "indexicality" to the former army barracks by continuing the "low-level urban texture set against the higher level blocks on the surrounding sides of the site." She sees the art center design as an "urban graft," a "second skin to the site."

Hadid's concept of the interior spaces "emancipates" the "coding" of the museum walls as the "the privileged and immutable vertical armature for the display of paintings," transforming the wall elements into a "versatile engine for the staging of exhibition effects." The center's spaces flow freely between interior and exterior; the redefined walls twist to become floors or ceilings.

A "further deviation from the classical composition of the wall" may be seen in the design's highly versatile exhibition system, which relies on a set of movable partitions that hang from ceiling ribs. "By constantly changing dimension and geometry," Hadid writes, "they adapt themselves to whatever curatorial role is needed."

"I love painting," Hadid said in a 2001 interview, "but the idea of art has changed from painting. The spaces in these centers don't have to be defined by the need for walls to hang pictures on. We can and should get away from the box, from ninety-degree angles."

High-tech meets tribal initiative

Indian architect Balkrishna Doshi is known for designs that rely on a sensitive adoption and refinement of modern architecture within an Indian context. Steeped in a life-long study of traditional Indian philosophy and ancient architectural texts, Doshi creates buildings that fuse contemporary architecture with ancient ideas.

The Hussain-Doshi Gufa gallery is a particularly apt example of this synthesis of high-tech and "tribal initiative." Designed to house a permanent exhibition of the paintings of contemporary Indian artist M. F. Hussain, "the Gufa" was built in Ahmedabad, India, in 1995 on the campus of the Centre for Environmental Planning and Technology. The architect has described the gallery as a fusion of art and architecture, because it is the result of a collaboration between Doshi and Hussain.

The structure is a configuration of underground cavelike spaces, capped by a striking series of connecting surface dome structures. The design evolved out of patterns of intersecting circles and ellipses. Doshi considers it "a human intervention and interpretation of a natural form." Indian writer Yatin Pandya has observed that the

The interior spaces of Hadid's National Centre for Contemporary Arts in Rome flow freely between interior and exterior. The walls twist to become floors or ceilings, transforming them into a "versatile engine for the staging of exhibition effects."

gallery recalls ancient rock-cut Buddhist sanctuaries with painted surfaces and sculpture.

The shell-like, ferro cement surface domes were designed with computers but built with traditional methods; no forms were used in their construction. The architect employed digital design technology to calculate and optimize structural stresses in the inch(3cm)-thick shells, but relied on semi-skilled workers, who built them on-site using hand tools. Projecting skylights and cutouts in these domes illuminate the interior spaces with shafts and spots of light, which is "reminiscent of the galaxy and stars."

The interior is a contiguous and amorphous space defined by wiremesh-and-mortar-lined, curvilinear walls and undulating floors. Leaning, irregular, "Stonehenge-like" columns further divide these spaces.

Feeding the electronic fauna

NOX is an architectural cooperative established by Dutch designers Lars Spuybroek and Maurice Nio. Known for its cutting-edge approach to design, the firm seeks to blur the lines separating media. Along with its architectural work, NOX has produced videos, installations, Internet content, and a magazine. NOX searches for hybrid forms through "a sort of genetic engineering where architecture has been crossbred with other media." The firm's architecture has been described as a supple combination of biological forms and "the metallic and electronic fauna of modern technologies."

NOX has created such high-concept projects as SoftSite, a liquid city generated by behavior on the Internet and projected on the facade of the Netherlands Architecture Institute, and the highly biomorphic D-Tower, "a coherent hybrid of different media where architecture is part of a larger interactive system of relationships," planned for the Dutch city of Doetinchem.

Spuybroek in particular is known for his theories on "liquid" and "flexible" architecture, and the idea that a building could be designed as a dynamic system of constant, computer-mediated interaction among users, environment, and building.

In 1997, Spuybroek created an interactive water pavilion for the Dutch Ministry of Transport's H2O eXPO that illustrates the main thrust of his architectural ideas. Called Freshwater, the structure was erected on the former industrial island of Neeltje Jans in the East Scheldt estuary.

Freshwater was actually half of a larger Water Pavilion that consisted of two interlocking sections; Kas Oosterhuis designed the second half, known as Saltwater. The entire structure was approximately 328 feet (100 meters) long. Spuybroek's pavilion was a luminous, organic deformation of the space, which offered a sharp contrast to Oosterhuis's more traditional, dark gray, tapered, and angular design.

Clad in stainless steel, Freshwater was a computer-generated design evolved through the fluid deformation of fourteen ellipses, which were spaced out over a length of more than 213 feet (65 meters) in the final structure. According to the architect, the design was based on the "metastable aggregation of architecture and information." It has been described as "a turbulent alloy of the hard and the weak, of human flesh, concrete and metal, interactive electronics and water."

Inside the building, which has no horizontal floors and no external relation to the horizon, "walking becomes akin to falling." The event brochure describes the situation this way: "In a simultaneous fusion of the walls, ground, and ceiling, the 'architecture-body' spreads out in a wavelike effect to absorb the territory.... [A]rchitecture becomes the interface for an active organization of space where visitors act upon a reactive architecture."

Spuybroek's idea was to make the forms as liquid as the water flowing past the pavilion. Mist and ocean spray intrude upon and inform the structure. Curved surfaces connect different elliptic sections throughout the structure. In the absence of clearly definable floors and walls, concepts like "interior" and "exterior" become blurred.

Ten computers support the building's interactive elements. Built-in sensors respond to the presence of visitors, initiating projections on their bodies, images, sounds, and shifts in lighting. The software receives input from such a range of sources that even the architect cannot predict the results.

Garofalo Architects

The Chicago-based architectural design practice founded by Douglas Garofalo in 1992 embraces both digital tools and computer networks as enabling technologies. The firm puts it this way on the company website: "It is our desire to translate the fluidity, flexibility, and complexity of contemporary technologies into built form."

Garofalo's collaboration with architects Greg Lynn and Michael McInturf on the design of the Korean Presbyterian Church of New York (1999) was entirely electronic: all three architects practiced in different cities and communicated their design ideas via a computer network. "By exploiting information transfers via electronic networks," the firm says, "we have been able to integrate geographically disparate parties into coherent and efficient design teams."

The Spring Prairie House project (below) involved a series of additions to a rambling farmhouse situated on 75 acres about 60 miles north of Chicago. The design called for several components comprising an additional 1,000 square feet, including bedrooms, bathrooms, a sunroom, a screened porch, an observation tower, and an animal barn.

Garofalo, along with project architect Julie Flohr, designed the additions to the 2,500-square-foot, barn-like building to produce a "comfortable retreat from the city for an extended family." The project required Garofalo and Flohr to compose structures that were "analogous to a small village, where everyone knows everyone else, but where privacy is possible."

With this design, Garofalo architects sought to open the complex to the surrounding "hybrid" landscape, which consisted of forest, prairie, lawn, and a garden. By draping the rectilinear structures with steel-framed curves, she created a design that simultaneously stands in striking contrast with the natural surroundings while flowing harmoniously into the landscape.

Flohr, too, embraces the computer as enabling technology. "Architecture, engineering, and design should be integrated," she told *Dwell* magazine's Virginia Gardiner in a 2003 interview. "For a long time, the architect had to sacrifice control of structure and fabrication. The computer enables a renaissance by reversing that predicament. The architect is back at the center of command."

chapter 6

an **utterance**
without a language

Hani Rashid and Lise Anne Couture find a new
architecture in the "dimensionless territories"

One of the abiding preoccupations of architect/designers Hani Rashid and Lise Ann Couture is the relationship between the digital and physical worlds. On the website for their New York–based firm, Asymptote Architects, they explain their notions of that relationship in modern architecture:

When speaking of architecture for the next millennium, one must consider two conditions: that the physical space of architecture as we have always known it…will without a doubt persevere; and that it will exist alongside the virtual architecture surfacing in the digital domain of the Internet. This new architecture of liquidity, flux, and mutability is predicated on technological advances fueled by the basic human desire to probe the unknown….

In their book, *Asymptote: Flux*, they go on to write: "Architecture for such fluid, dimensionless territories can only be an utterance, without language; a new architecture that is anticipatory, imperfect, and precisely misaligned."

As architects, teachers, designers, and virtual reality artists, the husband-and-wife team of Rashid and Couture use computers extensively to design buildings, urban spaces, and virtual environments. In 1988 they co-founded a collaborative practice that has become something of a standard bearer for digital architecture. "Asymptote" refers to a line whose distance from a given curve tends to zero. The idea of two lines that never meet was the perfect metaphor for Rashid and Couture's practice, which they describe as "…open ended, one that sees each project as part of a much larger body of work, a perpetual work in progress."

Like architect Greg Lynn and designer Karim Rashid (Hani's brother), the Asymptote team has used high-performance computers and sophisticated 3-D software to go beyond the limitations of the real world, but with their own, idiosyncratic aesthetic inspired not only by natural forms, but also by technology—even information itself.

It's safe to say that few architects or designers have used the power of the computer, both as a sophisticated drafting tool and as an instrument of artistic expression, to blur so compellingly the line between the real and the virtual. Applying digital design techniques to built structures, and architectural principles to digital spaces, Rashid, Couture, and company have plowed new ground, both literally and virtually.

"The computer is partially used for representational purposes," Couture said in a 2002 interview, "but it can also be a tool to help you undermine your preconceptions rather than allowing you to visualize them—an aid to entering new territory. It's not a fetishization of technology. It's more like, in our practice, we don't like to take things at face value."

An episodic architecture

In the late 1980s, the city of Los Angeles embarked on a search for a city monument, a kind of West Coast equivalent to the Statue of Liberty or St. Louis Gateway Arch. Then L.A. Mayor Tom Bradley char-

Designed by Hani Rashid and Lise Ann Couture, the Floriade Hydra Pier in Amsterdam reflects the cutting-edge thinking of this digital duo.

acterized the proposed structure as "a symbolic monument to welcome immigrants to America's shore."

Approximately 150 architects submitted proposals for the 1988 West Coast Gateway competition, among which were a giant bird, a massive baseball glove, and a towering fountain of water. But the selection committee expressed early on its belief that Los Angeles did not need a conventionally static monument. Committee chair Nick Patsaouras said that they wanted, rather, "a living, utilitarian reminder of our diverse cultural heritage . . . a landmark that would be a rallying point for the community."

If the committee wanted something dynamic, they surely got what they were looking for in the design they chose. Submitted by the newly formed Asymptote Architects, Steel Cloud was a twelve-story-high, four-block-long, glass-and-steel structure that would straddle the Hollywood Freeway in downtown L.A., and offer a physical interpretation of the 24-hours-a-day, 7-day-a-week pulse of the city and the technological heart that drives it.

The firm's website describes the design as an "episodic architecture" that was "inspired by optical phenomena, surveillance technology, telecommunications advances,

and the proliferation of information." Rashid and Couture expressed their ideas somewhat more poetically in a brochure issued at the time of the competition:

The answer lies sealed in the clouds so apparent over the edgeless horizon hung above the city of Los Angeles. To construct clouds, to construct the heavens—that is the task at hand. The steel clouds will occupy the invisible space above the freeway—the cacophonic world of the automobile reconciled with the symphonic raptures of culture. Theaters and libraries are the god houses. People of all origins will occupy these rooms, these people are the monument, not symbols or illusionary technologies. The steel clouds are traversing the horizon as an asymptote traverses infinity—the endless path forward into the new world.

Rising on piers set in the median strip, Steel Cloud would comprise a superstructure of paths and steel girders connecting a complex of buildings spanning a tensile bridge structure at one end and a compression bridge structure at the other. The Steel Cloud complex would include museums, libraries, restaurants, liquid crystal display screens,

The Guggenheim Virtual Museum consists of navigable three-dimensional spatial entities accessible on the Internet, as well as real-time interactive components at the various Guggenheim locations.

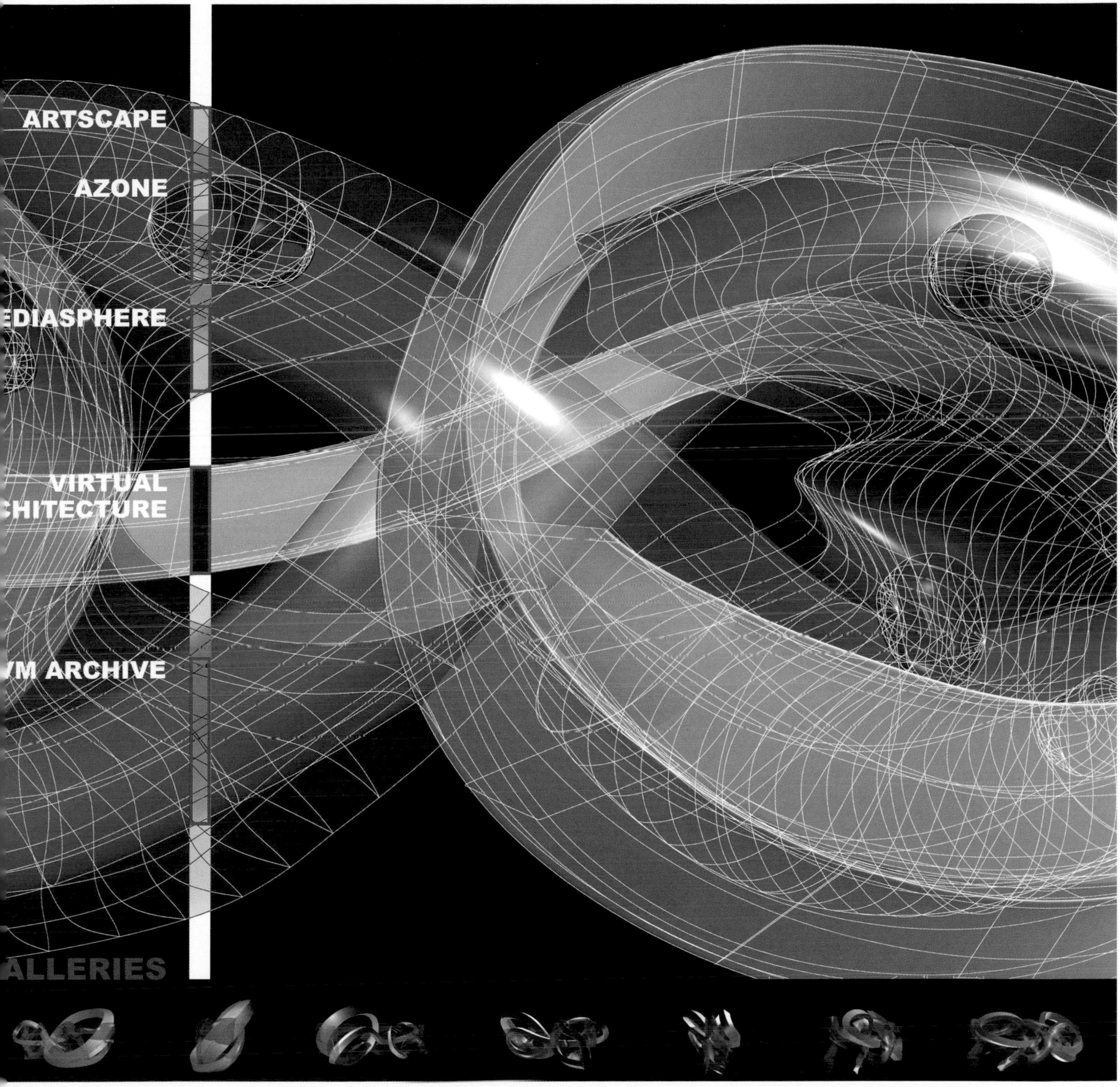

ARTSCAPE

AZONE

EDIASPHERE

VIRTUAL
CHITECTURE

VM ARCHIVE

ALLERIES

In 1998, the New York Stock
Exchange commissioned Rashid
and Couture's Asymptote to design
a three-dimensional, fully interactive,
virtual environment that closely
mirrored the physical and geographical
layout of the real trading floor.

movie screens, a theater, a sculpture garden, a painting gallery, a Park of Peace and Unity, and a "musical forest" of synthesizers that would transform the surrounding city sounds into music. The 140-foot-high (43 meter) aquariums, visible from the freeway, would represent the Pacific and Atlantic Oceans; scenes of Hollywood films would be projected on large silver screens; a laser beam would project an arc, ostensibly from L.A. across the Pacific to Tokyo Bay.

"This is an architecture for the territories devoid of perspective, depth, frames, or enclosure," Rashid has said of the design. During the 1980s, Rashid and Couture experimented with different media, including photographic darkroom drawing, video, sound, film, and multimedia computer software—much of which they seemed intent on incorporating into the monument.

Steel Cloud caused what a few literal-minded reporters described as a "storm of protests." Although some critics compared the proposed monument to Tatlin's unbuilt Monument to the Third International for Moscow and the Eiffel Tower in Paris, others saw the conglomeration of steel and multimedia as just another ugly, freeway pile-up. Still others expressed concerns about the structure's potential for actually causing acci-

dents by distracting motorists passing beneath it.

Patsaouras brushed aside such concerns, and promised that the structure would be "uplifting, giving one the feeling of soaring to the heavens."

The monument's superstructure was scheduled to be built in four phases, with the first targeted for completion in 1992 in time for the 500th anniversary of Christopher Columbus' voyage to America. But the $33 million project got bogged down in local politics. Landslides, riots, and a waning economy put the monument on permanent hold. Mayor Bradley left office in 1992. Although a group of Japanese investors approached Rashid and Couture about the possibility of constructing Steel Cloud near Tokyo Bay, the monument was ultimately left unbuilt. In 1994, the models and drawings for Steel Cloud were acquired by the FRAC Centre in Orleans, France, as part of its extensive architectural collection.

It has been observed that architectural competitions, such as the Los Angeles Gateway contest, have become more important as idea generators than as producers of built projects. Although Steel Cloud remains unbuilt, that fact may not hinder its influence in what Chicago-based architect John Hill calls the "architectural continuum." Writing for

his "Weekly Dose of Architecture" website, Hill put the importance of Steel Cloud in historical context:

In [Steel Cloud's] unbuilt nature lies its potential. It will become a piece of architectural influence and history, as much as Piranesi's imaginary views, Ledoux and Boullee's fantastical projects, Antonio Sant Elia's futuristic cities, Le Corbusier's League of Nations project and Rem Koolhaas's entry for the Très Grande Bibliotheque in Paris, among many others. The power of these projects lies in their strong conceptual clarity and ability to see beyond the present constraints of architectural practice.

Virtual architecture: prime protagonist
Rashid and Couture's controversial, high-concept design for the West Coast Gateway competition launched Asymptote into the spotlight, but it was their ability to transfer their architectural skills and vision into the virtual space of a computer environment nearly a decade later that put them in the history books.

In the mid-1990s, the New York Stock Exchange (NYSE) set out to integrate its vast storehouse of computer data into a single, user-friendly, computer-accessible system. The project had begun primarily with a technological focus, but the Silicon Valley engineers assigned to organize the information visually were having trouble coming up with an effective navigation scheme.

The NYSE contacted Asymptote in 1998 to consult on the project. By this time Rashid and Couture had acquired a reputation for exploring the relationship between the digital and physical worlds. They had, in fact, been experimenting with an architectural approach to the design of virtual spaces, and so the idea of architects taking on a project more typically assigned to website designers did not seem especially novel to the pair. "We approached it as if it was a traditional architectural project," they recalled during a recent talk at the Museum of Modern Art.

Using an architectural approach, Asymptote designed a three-dimensional, fully interactive, virtual environment that closely mirrors the physical and geographical layout of the real trading floor. Asymptote's 3-D Trading Floor (3DTF) is the financial world's first large-scale, virtual operational control center. It collects transactional and network activity data, and displays it on a high-resolution video wall in the form of an

animated, real-time, 3-D representation of the physical trading floor.

Asymptote describes the project this way:

The design of the virtual trading floor began as a reinterpretation and transformation of the existing physical trading environment. The architectural idealization had to provide absolute flexibility; particularly to accommodate the data feeds that would eventually be programmed into it. The modeling also needed to provide for consistent shifts in scale, enhanced levels of detail, and the insertion of numerous other kinetic virtual objects. Thus, the actual trading floor had to be reconfigured for several reasons: the model had to function in real time, which produced high technological demands; and an economy of forms was necessary to process and animate extremely large quantities of data.

The fully interactive 3DTF consolidates several data streams and presents them in a virtual environment that allows for the manipulation of spatial and temporal dimensions. In other words, in the 3DTF, users

Asymptote's 3-D Trading Floor is the financial world's first large-scale, virtual operational control center. It collects transactional and network activity data and displays it on a high-resolution video wall in the form of an animated, real-time, 3-D representation of the physical trading floor.

can be in more than one place—scale, points of view—at the same time. The system employs icons, color, and animation to alert NYSE operations staff about unusual business and systems activity. The staff can also "drill down" through the virtual floors and walls of the environment to examine the operation of key subsystems.

Stock prices, news, indexes, and live video from major television networks are constantly flowing into the virtual environment, where they are presented in real time on ticker bands and video displays on the "walls" of the space. Virtual trade booths, arranged in the same position they occupy in the real world, are set up on the "floor" of the 3DTF, providing users with a familiar layout. An interactive 3-D graph sits in the virtual floor, which allows for instant replay of graph-events that occur in the stock market.

"The idea was to create a visual environment through which traders can navigate, analyze, and act upon at a glance," Rashid and Couture have said. "Trade actions are very dynamic. What happens on the trade floor gets immediately broadcast through

the media, information on which the market reacts, and then quickly translated into orders on the floor."

Asymptote used Alias|Wavefront's Maya software, the Cosmo Worlds Virtual Reality Markup Language (VRML), Adobe Photoshop, and Adobe Premiere to build the interface. The Israeli firm RT-SET, which specializes in virtual sets for TV election coverage, developed the real-time animation and rendering software that generates the virtual world.

The success of the virtual trading floor led to a corollary, real-world commission. The NYSE needed to establish an access point to the 3DTF, and it called upon Asymptote to design a kind of theater of operations, which the NYSE called The Advanced Trading Floor Operation Center. When it was launched in 1999, the system was powered by six Onyx2s graphics visualization supercomputers from Silicon Graphics (who reportedly first suggested the 3-D project to the NYSE back in 1994), 43 PixelVision high-resolution, flat-panel monitors, and some highly innovative applications. The screens seem to float in front of a

curved blue glass wall, a curved and winding work surface. Ribbons of text on various surfaces capture the different "flows" that encompass the Stock Exchange trading floor.

The 3DTF was initially designed primarily to enable the NYSE to supervise its trading environment, but the project later evolved to include a large-scale Internet initiative and a television broadcasting environment. According to Rashid and Couture, these "mutations and elaborations" of the project have further architectural implications "as the virtual realm slowly usurps the real trading floor as a 'place.'" In *Asymptote: Flux*, they write:

The fact that the general public will soon be able to navigate a virtual trading floor, check stock news and valuations, make trades, and meander about at will, is unprecedented and begs the question, What actually constitutes an architectural experience and presence? And for those who do inhabit and are familiar with the real trading floor, what new insights into their environment can be attained and how might these alter their understanding of

Asymptote designed the NYSE's Advanced Trading Floor Operation Center, a state-of-the-art command center that serves as the backdrop to media events staged from the floor of the NYSE and is a means to showcase the exchange's technological advances and capabilities. A primary element of the center is a large backlit surface of curved and tilted blue glass fitted with up to sixty high-resolution, flat-screen monitors and nine other screens that display the virtual trading floor.

what constitutes architecture.

Asymptote's work on the 3DTF led to another commission in cyberspace. In 1999, the Guggenheim Foundation in New York called upon Rashid and Couture's firm to design an Internet-based museum to "house" digital art for the Solomon R. Guggenheim Museum. When completed, the Guggenheim Virtual Museum may be the largest three-dimensional, interactive environment of its kind. The purpose of this museum in cyberspace is not merely to convert paintings and videos into digital objects, but also to serve as a home for a growing number of modern works that are digital in nature—both art and architecture—that can only be viewed on computers.

Promotional literature on the project describes it this way:

The Guggenheim Virtual Museum will not only provide global access to all Guggenheim museums, including typical museum services, amenities, archives, and collections, but also provide a unique and compelling spatial environment to be experienced by the virtual visitor. In addition, the virtual museum is an ideal space for deploying and experiencing art and events created specifically for the interactive digital medium. Here, simultaneous viewing and participation are possible by an audience around the globe. As envisioned by Asymptote, the Guggenheim Virtual Museum will emerge from the fusion of information space, art, commerce, and architecture to become one of the most important virtual buildings of the twenty-first century.

Like the 3DTF, the virtual museum will also have a physical presence, in the form of a 43-by-24-foot (13.1m x 7.3m) video wall at the entrance to the Guggenheim's SoHo branch. Asymptote has employed software tools from Alias|Wavefront, Adobe, and Macromedia, to build this three-dimensional, interactive environment.

Unlike the 3DTF, the form and structure of which Rashid and Couture see as "gamelike," as in video games, or "…data-delivery mechanisms through which one has to respond quickly and efficiently" the Virtual Guggenheim is an environment with an entirely different mandate:

The Guggenheim Virtual Museum…. Is a place for the flaneur, the wanderer, to borrow from Beaudelaire. The virtual museum is meant to act as an architectural experience tied to wonder, awe, and memory, a collection of datascapes that one might get lost in or, at the very least, in which one can enjoy a certain kind of delirium.

This idea that the digital realm we sometimes call virtual reality is a "place" is what makes it possible for architects to ply their trade there. Matthew Drutt, associate curator of the Guggenheim and leader of the virtual museum's design team, has said, "The most important defining element is the notion that the virtual museum is a place, a space. It's not a dynamic graphic representation of text and image." In other words, the Virtual Guggenheim, like the 3DTF, is not a page. In the hands of designers like Rashid and Couture, it possesses a kind of destabilized spatiality. Even concepts like walls, floors, inside, and outside may be accepted or ignored in this fluid terrain of infinite possibility.

Furthermore, these virtual terrains are not limited even by the hard drives on which they exist. Through an effectively limitless ability to link with other spaces on the Web, digital architects have at their disposal an utterly boundless territory.

Their ground-breaking work on the Virtual Guggenheim and the 3D Trading Floor have put Rashid and Couture on the bleeding edge of digital architecture—or perhaps more appropriately in their case, virtual architecture. They characterize it as an "evolving discipline that

Asymptote's work on the 3DTF led to their development in 1999 of the Guggenheim Virtual Museum, a museum in cyberspace that acts as "an architectural experience tied to wonder, awe, and memory, a collection of datascapes that one might get lost in or, at the very least, in which one can enjoy a certain kind of delirium."

results from the convergence of data mapping and simulation, digital form making, information architecture, and virtual reality constructs and theory." Like Greg Lynn, they seem to be drawn by the digital realm's ability to transcend heretofore immutable architectural values. Where traditional architecture is based on permanence and geometric certainty, virtual architecture "utilizes digital technologies to augment real events, time, and space."

Of the influence of computers on their own practice and approach to architecture and design, they write:

At Asymptote the computer increasingly plays a vital role in all phases of design, from sketch to engineering and through to implementation. In this way our work is influenced by digital tools and the new theories emerging today because of them. Virtual architecture…undoubtedly influences the ways we now understand space, form, movement, and geometry. Virtual architecture is for the moment manifest mostly within virtual space, and the Internet is a prime protagonist in creating entirely new forms of "dwellings;" but virtual architecture might very well constitute the pioneer effort in forging new forms of real habitation…

Real space
Of course, Rashid and Couture do use computer technologies to conceptualize and build on solid ground. One of Asymptote's most striking real-world designs—one of their few built structures as of this writing—is the Foriade Hydra-Pier, a municipal pavilion constructed in 2002 in the city of Haarlemmermeer in the Netherlands. Built originally to host the Foriade 2002 World Horticulture Exhibition and promote the host city to international visitors, the building is an enclosed multimedia exhibition space surrounded by a

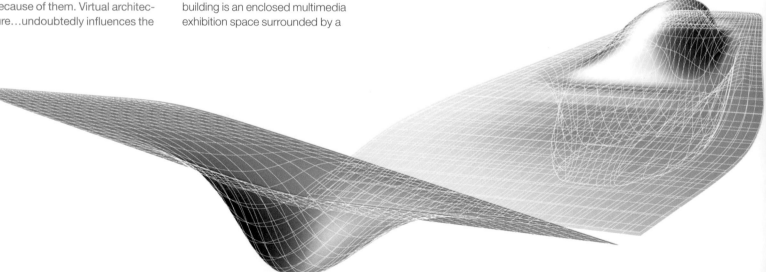

Rashid and Couture are known for drawing inspiration for their designs from a wide range of sources not traditionally associated with architecture—everything from organic systems to sporting equipment, honeycombs to aircraft interiors. For the Hydra-Pier, they drew their inspiration from the large-bodied airplanes arriving and departing a nearby airport. As seen in this computer rendering, the overall form of the chrome-silver pavilion is similar to a creased airplane wing.

One of Asymptote's most striking real-world designs is the Foriade Hydra-Pier, a municipal pavilion constructed in 2002 in the city of Haarlemmermeer in the Netherlands. Built originally to host the Foriade 2002 World Horticulture Exhibition and promote the host city to international visitors, the building is an enclosed multimedia exhibition space surrounded by a large deck.

The Hydra-Pier is separated into two parts: one overhangs and shelters an outdoor landscaped space; the other, floating on the lake, encloses a multimedia space for public events and other functions.

large deck. A permanent structure, it is the home of a technology and art display.

The Hydra-Pier is located near the Schipol airport, adjacent to the city of Amsterdam, in a country setting that contrasts sharply with nearby urban scenes. This setting is essentially an artificial one: reclaimed land that, until about 150 years ago, lay under five meters of seawater. It was pumped dry by 19th-century Dutch engineers, who kept the sea at bay with a series of "water walls" and transformed the site into habitable land; many of the original pumping stations are still in existence.

Rashid and Couture are known for drawing inspiration for their designs from a wide range of sources not traditionally associated with architecture—everything from organic systems to sporting equipment, honeycombs to aircraft interiors. For the Hydra-Pier, they seem to have reached skyward for their inspiration to the large-bodied airplanes passing frequently overhead as they arrive and depart from Schipol airport, but they also had their feet firmly on the watery ground. The overall form of the chrome-silver pavilion is similar to a creased airplane wing, stretched out from the shore of the Haarlemmermeer Bos Lake, with half its length over the water.

The Hydra-Pier is separated into two parts; one overhangs and shelters an outdoor landscaped space, the other, floating on the lake, encloses a multimedia space for public events and other functions.

The two inclined metallic planes of its roof are drenched with water continuously pumped and circulated over the surface, pooled in clear-glazed concave sections, and spilling down the sides of the structure. In fact, visitors enter along a bridge that passes through two cascading water-walls. As water flows over the building's glass walls, light casts a running liquid pattern on the floor. This controlled flow, Rashid and Couture write in *Asymptote: Flux*, "fuses with the winglike structure to create reflective, glistening, seemingly fluid surfaces.... The resultant spatial condition plays on the displacement of water relative to sea level and alludes to the artificial condition of the Hydra-Pier's natural setting."

Thus, the Hydra-Pier serves as a symbol of Holland's tenuous relationship with the surrounding sea. In the words of Asymptote, "The Hydra-Pier is an architecture articulating the struggle between land and water, nature and technological artifice."

It also serves as an example of Asymptote's ongoing exploration of the relationship between the real and the virtual. "In our work," Rashid explained in a recent interview, "we are trying to figure out how to build a blurred space between two realities. If we do a physical project, like the Floriade Hydra-Pier, we're out to discover ways in which that project can become virtual. It's a 'real' project, but if you stream water on the roof and it makes the skin of the building look ephemeral, will the result start to change against the sky and the light, and will it then become

For the Knoll A3 Furniture Systems project, the architects at Asymptote used their digital design approach to "rethink the office landscape." Rashid and Couture found inspiration for this system of office cubicles in sports apparel and sports gear, designing each module to "fit" and protect the body. The shell is composed of removable translucent nylon fabric stretched over rounded aluminum frames.

With their orange, yellow, and blue accents, the movable A3-modules are almost tent-like. Grouped together, the organic form factors of the modules allow for office planners and designers to group them to create alcoves, breakout spaces, impromptu gathering spots, and meeting areas.

a kind of virtualized object?"

For the Knoll A3 Furniture Systems project, Asymptote brought its dazzling digital design approach to a project that couldn't have been more pedestrian: a system of office cubicles. The idea was to create a modular, reconfigurable system that could respond to the behavior of the office workers who use them.

Architects by background, Rashid and Couture approached this industrial design problem from a "spatial and environmental" perspective. In their book, they recall their initial reaction to the commission:

The project was seen as a valuable opportunity to rethink the dynamics of the office landscape: How do people interact in quasi-wireless, digitally equipped environments? How can one have a sense of privacy while also feeling like part of a larger community? What are the new emotionally charged forms and materials that we surround ourselves with on a daily basis? How can these be employed to create vibrant and interesting work environments and furnishings?

How can a desire for versatility and flexibility be accommodated while at the same time maintaining a high level of efficiency? Can this be achieved while still bringing a sense of order and dignity to our workspaces?

The answer to these questions, for Asymptote at least, was the A3 Furniture System. The A3 workstation is a 36-square-foot (11 square meters) freestanding biomorphic cockpit composed of soft, molded curves. The shell is composed of removable translucent nylon fabric stretched over rounded aluminum frames. With their orange, yellow, and blue accents, the movable modules are almost tentlike. Mobile pedestal units can double as secondary work surfaces. All accessories, including letter trays, pencil cups, and a coat hook, are anchored to the frame. The design of the overhead storage was inspired by the forms of airliner storage bins. Call the A3 the anti-cube.

"It was imperative that the new workstation no longer feel impersonal and 'machined,'" Rashid and Couture write, "but rather become a desirable, human-scaled place to inhabit."

Rashid and Couture are said to have found inspiration for the A3 System in sports apparel and sports gear, designing the modules to "fit" and protect the body. They used semi-transparent screens to help achieve a balance of openness, lightness, and privacy. The workstations have a side entrance instead of traditional front or back openings. Grouped together, the organic form factors of the modules allow for office planners and designers to group them to create alcoves, breakout spaces, impromptu gathering spots, and meeting areas.

"The A3 reflects the readings we made concerning not only the way we communicate and inhabit," Rashid said in a 2001 interview, "but also the desires and wants we have when we are able to freely maneuver our way through data, art, relationships and so on."

the "poster boy"
for **blobism**

Karim Rashid sets out to change the world

Karim Rashid's Oh Chair is an inexpensive, stackable, soft plastic chair, utterly devoid of angles.

Most modern industrial designers rely on computers, at least to some extent. It's a wearingly competitive market, and not many could afford to ignore the speed and other advantages those technologies afford. But few cyber-savvy designers have carried the digital banner higher than Karim Rashid. The New York–based industrial designer has embraced the technology as an elemental means to his artistic ends. In the computer, he has found the perfect tool for creating "tactile surfaces" that provide "comfortable, engaging, physical experiences." Moreover, among the fluid forms that thrive in the virtual design environment he has discovered a vehicle for bringing humanity and diversity to mass production.

Rashid's website proclaims, "…I am the 'artist of real issues'…who mediates between industry and the user, between self-expression and desire, between production technologies and human social behavior, between commerce and everyday life."

An unabashed manufacturer's designer, Rashid has written, "Design is not so much about self-expression as it is about being conversant in the languages of engineering, marketing, and management." And yet, for Rashid, computer design technology is not merely a production tool, but an enabling force in an age all but empty of once common craftsmanship. In his book, *Karim Rashid: I Want to Change the World*, he writes:

As computer technology becomes more sophisticated, it promises levels of refinement in design that will compensate for the lack of craft skills, which have faded since the Industrial Revolution rendered the guild obsolete…. Increasingly, our tools are digital, and designers are poised to harness the capabilities of this new equipment with which they can create beautiful, useful objects that manifest a uniqueness and variety that the Machine Age stamped out.

Rashid has been called the "poster boy for **blobism**," and he is credited with coining the term "**blobject**," which he used to name a couch he designed with sophisticated Bézier raster software. **Blobism**, he says, emerged from a "casualization of shape" that is being driven by technology and generating a nascent milieu that he calls "the new softscape." This change, he writes, is manifesting in our everyday objects, and even our selves:

The world around us seems to be perpetually getting softer. Our objects are softer, our cars are rounder, our computers are **blobier**, and even our bodies are fatter…. The digital age, the information society, the global village, and the leisure culture are all acronyms that symbolize a changing physical world where "soft" denotes our landscape. Soft is a metaphor for our forever-changing, ever-vast organic system…. I have aggressively softened objects for our contemporary culture because soft means human, friendly, approachable, and comfortable. Soft is an extension of our bodies—tactile, flexible, playful, and engaging. Soft is not decorative or embellishment if it relates directly to the subject at hand—us, interacting with things on a daily basis. The danger is that if "soft" becomes a style, then everything will be **blobified**....

Rashid sees **blobism** as a distinctly American phenomenon. The United States, he says, has "created a kind of digital language of **blobifying** our world, physically and immaterially." What he calls the "**blobject** movement" began in the United States, he says, thanks to a handful of designers with a great interest in organic forms and the technology that allows them to "morph, undulate, twist, torque, blend, and metaball our concepts." He traces the movement's origins back to the 1940s and 1950s, to designers such as the Eameses, Isamu Noguchi, Harry Bertoia, and Zeisel. Although they lacked the ability to perfectly articulate their ideas with computers, they started the **blob** rolling.

Like the postwar designers who exploited new materials developed for the military to realize their curvilinear visions, Rashid finds inspiration in synthetics. In a 2003 interview, Rashid told *Interior Design* magazine, "I like to work with almost all materials, but I must say that I love plastics, because to me they are the most prescient, most flexible, and complex of materials. They have incredible potential."

In his book, Rashid treats his readers to what amounts to a paean to plastic:

Polymers, such as synthetic rubbers, santoprenes, evoprenes, polyolifens, silicones, translucencies, transparencies, all contribute to the new softness of our products. Multiple materials on a singular object by new technologies such as dual-durometer molding, co- and triple-injection enrich the interface with our bodies.... Materials can now flex, change, morph, shift color, cool and heat...due to the Smart material movement...materials that communicate and give us feedback.

There's an irony in the fact that what makes Rashid's sinuous organic forms possible is a combination of these kinds of high-tech materials and the computer-driven manufacturing systems that shape virtually anything he conceives in cyberspace with real-world laser cutters or high-powered water jets.

As of this writing, Rashid has designed hundreds of objects in a host of materials. He has designed **blob-shaped** TVs, stereos, and DVD players for Sony, **blobby** blister packs for Prada, and a hot-pink Ultrasuede modular sofa for Galerkin. He has created furniture, coat racks, mailboxes, perfume packaging, CD players, lighting, tableware, and even clothing. He has designed retail spaces and restaurants, satellite-guided jogging shoes, crematorium urns, and etched crystal vases. But he is perhaps most famous for two of his earliest designs, both of which, though not strictly "evolved" in the manner of Greg Lynn's animated **blobs**, evince a similarly technology-driven biomorphic sensibility.

Rashid's "Garbo" trashcan is an industrial design icon. The Garbino pictured here is a smaller version of its predecessor.

Sensual minimalism

In Karim Rashid's world, everyday objects matter, and he believes that, increasingly, they matter in our world, too. In 2000, he told *Time* magazine, "The more time we spend in front of computer screens, the more the look of our coffee cup takes on added importance." Consequently, Rashid seeks to infuse his designs with what he calls a "sensual minimalism." He explained the concept in a 2001 interview: "Sensual minimalism is about the idea that there is very little in the work about embellishment. It's just what's necessary. At the same time it's a little off, a little human, a little organic. So it's sensual. It has that engagement."

One of the best examples of this notion is his Garbo wastebasket, created for Umbra in 1995, and one of the first designs from Rashid's own firm. According to one story, Paul Rowan and Les Mandelbaum of the Buffalo-based Umbra asked Rashid to "put his mind to the ubiquitous problem of the household wastebasket." According to another, Rashid approached Umbra with the Garbo concept, and the company's

The phenomenally successful Oh Chair was followed by the Ya Table, named as a play on a Canadian expression: "Oh ya." (Rashid was raised in Canada.) Also made of injection-molded polypropylene, Rashid said that he designed the soft and organic Ya Table because "everyone who wanted the Oh Chair wanted a table to go with it."

initial interest was lukewarm. Rashid persisted, the story goes, and the result was a thirteen-inch (33cm) -tall, five-gallon (22.7 liter) -capacity wastebasket molded of high-impact polypropylene, with a matte finish of translucent colors—and something of a blockbuster for Umbra.

According to Rashid, he developed the initial concept for the can with Pilot Fineliner drawings in his sketchbooks. He later scanned the images into his computer, where he could rotated, spin, and generally manipulate them in the 3-D virtual design environment. He pulled and stretched a simple circle to form the walls of the can, and employed a "saddle" or "butterfly" cut along the rim to create the curving lines of the opening. Into these curves he fit the negative space of the handles. The final design exudes Rashid's sensual minimalism, but with less artsy considerations for the practicalities of a mass-produced product. The Garbos don't stick together when stacked in a warehouse, for example. And Rashid rounded the interior bottom of the finished can for easier cleaning—a feature of which he is known to be particularly proud.

The Garbo name reportedly emerged from a brainstorming session at Umbra. It was an unnamed salesman, the company says, who offered the play on "garbage" and the name of the late, great Hollywood star, of whose curvy form its shape is reminiscent.

Umbra has sold millions of Garbos, and continues to produce them. The company later issued a smaller version of the Garbo, the Garbino, created for the Japanese and European markets where the original was generally thought to be too large, and a larger one, the Garbanzo, a swing-top kitchen garbage can. There's even a Garbowl: a fruit bowl with lines similar to the original. Today, the Garbo is used as a clothes hamper, a flower vase, an umbrella stand, a Champagne cooler, and even a horse feeder. Umbra now describes the Garbo line as an "alternative storage medium."

Rashid's sensual, biomorphic design elevated the common, plastic wastebasket to icon status. The Garbo is now in numerous permanent museum collections.

Recast classic
Danish designer Verner Panton is credited with the design of the first single-form injection-molded plastic chair, called the Stacking Chair, which he created in 1960. Rashid's version of this venerable object became another iconic blockbuster. In 1999, Umbra was in the market for a product that would help the company to broaden its image beyond the picture frames, dish racks, toothbrush holders, and wastebaskets for which it was then best known. Rashid's concept for an inexpensive, stackable, soft plastic chair was just what they were looking for.

According to Umbra, Rashid was eating lunch at "Le Jardin something or other" when he noticed how dreary the chairs were. It was "a fancy yuppie brunch place with $8 chairs," Rashid recalled. "I resolved that if there was one thing in the culture I would recast this would be it."

Rashid began his design with a quick sketch on a restaurant napkin. Working later on his computer, he sculpted a simple chair with soft curves, devoid of angles, building the piece around negative space— creating the holes first, so to speak. It was an approach with a practical as well as artistic application. As one retailer enthused in his catalog description, "Placed for design but optimized for flexibility and comfort, the spaces give the chair the feeling of art as well as decreasing its volume to make it easier to carry around and ship."

The result was the Oh Chair, a soft, inexpensive chair of virgin polypropylene and steel tubing, named for the sound of a meditative mantra—*Ohm*). Another artsy piece designed with prosaic practicalities, the Oh's materials make it resistant to stains, environmental damage, and wear and tear. According to one story, Rashid changed the design slightly at the last second, making it wider by three inches (eight centimeters) "after seeing the guys in the factory with their big asses." Rashid

recalled in an interview, "European chairs are too delicate. America needs bigger, stronger, more casual furniture. If you meet the American criteria, you have a global product."

In her review of the chair for *ArtByte*, artist Dike Blair saw the design very much in the tradition of Charles and Ray Eames and Eero Saarinen. "However," Blair wrote, "the negative space ovals in the body of the Oh, which provide graphic presence and light weight, could not, and would not, have been executed with '40s technology and aesthetic. They require advanced plastics technology and speak of CAD. The Oh's smoky-blue translucent plastic body is also very contemporary (somewhat iMacesque). It seems to say, 'I may be cheap, but I'm not hiding anything.'"

The Oh Chair was followed by the Ya Table. (Apparently, the name is a play on a Canadian expression: "Oh ya." Rashid was raised in Canada.) Also made of injection-molded polypropylene, Rashid said that he designed the soft and organic Ya Table because "everyone who wanted the Oh Chair wanted a table to go with it."

The Oh Chair is another manifestation of Rashid's abiding interest in bringing an individual creative vision to the design of everyday things. During a speech he gave to students at New York's Pratt Institute , he talked about his goal of designing common objects that were beautiful

Rashid designed his Kareames injection-molded plastic chairs as an homage to the great Charles and Ray Eames. The design, created in 2000 for Magis, suggests the molded plywood of the Eames's celebrated "potato chip" chair.

as well as practical. "I wanted to make beautiful, elegant, sculptural household objects with a very low price point," he said. "I always believed in design as not creating something elite, but something everyone can afford. My original goal was for these forty-dollar chairs to cost twenty dollars."

The Oh Chair has earned Rashid comparison with legendary designers Charles and Ray Eames. Rashid's connection with these designers is apparent in his homage to their molded plywood "potato chip chairs," which exemplified the organic impulse of the post–WWII period: his injection-molded plastic Kareames, designed in 2000 for Magis.

Blobjects, globjects, and the superblob

Rashid usually gets the credit for coining the term **"blobject"** and for introducing it into the design vocabulary. It seems likely that he first applied it to a chair that he designed for an exhibit at the Sandra Gering Gallery in New York. At the time, *NY Arts* magazine compared his chairs to the 1950s horror film monster:

Rashid created his Kapsule chair for
the Philadelphia-based Bozart. This
bloblike, molded plastic children's seat
also functions as a storage unit/toy box.
Rashid later developed Kapsule Tables
with the same storage feature to
complement the chairs.

"...the tinted or transparent chairs seem to pulsate and glide like man-o-war jellyfish. Curiously they are made from rigid polyethylene but the unorthodox use to which it has been put suggests a living organism." He also used it to name a limited-edition couch created in 1999. The lozenge-shaped piece was made of two-toned, double-dipped, soft polyvinyl chloride, and limited to a run of 250. Only five of Rashid's **Globjects** were made. Similarly pill-shaped, this greenish piece was made of an electro luminescent sheet of soft polyurethane resin and cables.

Rashid's **Superblob** is essentially a set of high-tech beanbag chairs with bio-ergonomic qualities. The group of sculpted and padded **blobs** includes a five-seat sofa, a two-seater, an armchair, and a chaise lounge. Each component is made from elastic fabric, and filled with polystyrene pearls. And each

has a shell seat in transparent yellow or fluorescent pink.

Of his **Superblob** pieces, Rashid has said, "It is a couture project. The product belongs to the category of informals, because its structure is not rigid, but the cuts that shape the upholstery make the forms perfectly sculpted. **Superblob** was conceived for a world without corners and is destined to increase the informality of a habitat. The forms of the furnishings approach those of the body to create a symbiosis and become extensions of the floor."

Superblob was designed for Italian manufacturer Edra, which describes the **Superblob** as furniture that "takes advantage of cutting-edge materials and translates them into a humanistic message of relaxed seating. The **Superblob** is a casual approach to the function of sitting down that

defies social convention." (The original beanbag chair, Il Sacco, also debuted in Italy; it was created in 1968 by Italian designers Piero Gatti, Cesare Paolini, and Franco Teodoro.)

The Kapsule chair, designed for the Philadelphia-based Bozart, is a **bloblike** children's seating design that also functions as a storage unit/toy box. Manufactured in molded plastic, the Kapsule's design included an easily opened "portal" for storing toys. The literature on the piece proclaims that the design "couples elevated design with inexpensive materials—both of which serve as a vehicle for introducing fine design and fun into the lives of children." Rashid later developed Kapsule Tables with the same storage feature to complement the chairs.

Rashid also brought a distinctly biomorphic sensibility to his package designs for Issey Miyake. The

For his Bopp Vase and Kissing Candlesticks (designed for Nambé), Rashid opted for classic crystal, but still managed to suggest the organic.

Rashid switched from plastic to metal in his design of Nambé's Kissing Salt and Pepper Shakers (shown left with kissing bud vases). According to one story, the company installed 12 machines just to crank out Karim-designed objects.

Japanese fashion company is well known for living at the bleeding edge of concept packaging, a perfect home for Rashid's Torso, Bust, and Spine bags. Made of flat sheets of polypropylene with injection poly-olefin handles, the semi-transparent shopping bags curve to suggest the human forms their names invoke. (Spine has a silver nylon strap.)

In 2002, Rashid created a perfume bottle for Issey Miyake's summer fragrance. The design was really two bottles: the inner container was a sleek cone; the outer, a fluid, organic shape. The injection-molded plastic bottle's misty, graduated color made the entire object seem to float.

His obvious love of plastic notwithstanding, Rashid maintains a similar fluidity of form in the famous metal salt and pepper shakers, candlesticks, and dinnerware he designed for Nambé. The New Mexico–based foundry commissioned Rashid in 1994 to design a set of curvilinear, aluminum-alloy tableware. The project began, Rashid recalled in an interview, with his investigation of the capabilities of aerospace computer numeric controlled machines. The story goes that Rashid helped the company to

shift its operations from strictly hand-labor–intensive practices, such as sand casting of metal and hand blowing of glassware, to modern production technologies and techniques. Nambé would eventually install 12 such machines to crank out Karim-designed objects.

"My goal is to create products by machines, where we can eliminate laborious, repetitive motions," Rashid said in an interview. "By using new technology and production techniques, we will never have to put another person on an assembly line."

Even in the Nambé crystal pieces—his Bopp Vase and Kissing Candlesticks, for example—Rashid manages to suggest the organic. Named for the Hale Bopp Comet, the Bopp Vases "flare upward and appear to bend into whirlwinds of crystal," in the words of the manufacturer. And the candlesticks seem to sway against each other.

For Wavelength, which he designed for Nienkämper, Rashid used undulating curves as his theme. His two- and three-seat armless sofas and benches, and individual lounge chairs with arms, were designed to provide seating for

In 2002, Rashid created his **Blob** Lights for Foscarini. The globular light fixtures were manufactured in polycarbonate plastic, and designed for floor, shelves, wall, or ceiling.

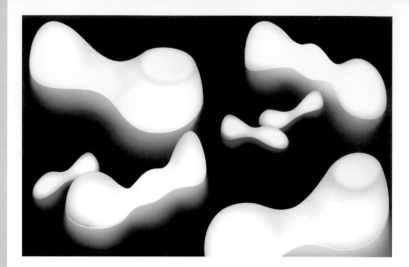

Rashid's famous Wavelength furniture, designed for Nienkämper, offers undulating curves that, when the individual sofas, benches, and lounge chairs are standing side by side, "continue metaphorically, ad infinitum."

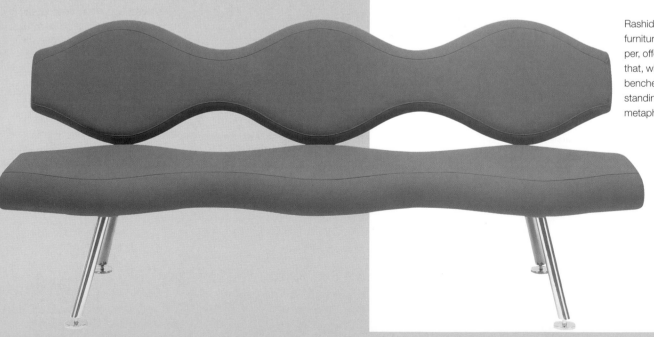

airports, public lobbies, retail outlets, and other public spaces. Each piece is upholstered, with polished aluminum bases. The Wavelength pieces can stand as individual units, or stand side-by-side to form rows of seating, creating waves that can "continue metaphorically, ad infinitum."

The **blob** moniker appeared again in 2002, when Foscarini introduced Rashid's globular **Blob** Lights. Manufactured in polycarbonate plastic, the white or orange-yellow half-globes were designed for the floor, placed on shelves or mounted to the wall or ceiling. The large one, the **Blob** XL, was designed to double as a seat or small table.

In his Soft Collection, Rashid's first series of designs for George Kovacs Lighting, the **blob** becomes a glowing orb. Made of hand-blown, tinted Murano glass mounted on polished chrome bases of varying length, the series combines four basic forms into sixteen different table, floor, and suspension lamps.

The Soft series is much admired, both as a successful design, and for its modularity, which contributes to manufacturing efficiency. "Individually and together, the shapes hold their proportions well," observed designer Nasir Kassamali, writing in *Business Week*. "The most compelling part of this design is the systems approach that the designer

In Rashid's Soft Collection, created for George Kovacs Lighting, the **blob** becomes a glowing orb. Made of hand-blown tinted Murano glass mounted on polished chrome bases of varying length, the series combines four basic forms into sixteen different table, floor, and suspension lamps.

took, bringing efficiency as well as elegance to its production."

Global energy

In 1999 Rashid created the winning design for Consolidated Edison's Commemorative Millennium Manhole Cover. *New York Times* architecture critic Herbert Muschamp described the 32-inch (81cm) -wide, 314-pound (142kg), cast iron cover as a "freshly minted metropolitan coin: graphically crisp, emphatically abstract, but with an abstraction's subliminal power to evoke a multitude of images."

Working in the virtual design space of his computer, Rashid "morphed, bulged, and mutated" a Manhattan street grid into a stylized, globe-shaped pattern. He explained at the time that the swelling criss-cross pattern represented the interplay between "data and energy" and presented the illusion of "earth erupting into a sphere." His design, which he called "Global Energy," was intended to represent New York as the center of an international data network.

Rashid sounded like a cross between a computer geek and a visionary artist when he commented on the process through which he had created the design. "We are in the digital age of Internet access and advanced communications," he said, "which is really a metaphor for being globally connected. Through a special software program, I was able to create a pattern…that would have been extremely labor intensive and time consuming if done by hand.

Today the technology has become so seamless that I created more than 30 separate proposals for this project. I couldn't have done that using traditional design methods."

The manhole covers would eventually replace around 150 of Con Ed's 250,000 manhole covers in the city of New York and Westchester County. A display version of the design cost $10,000 to produce, but the rest would cost about $200 each. Rashid later re-imagined his bulging grid pattern for the face of his OP Pocket Watch.

Blobworlds

It was probably inevitable that Rashid would stretch his amoeboid aesthetic beyond individual objects. Rashid's art installation, Pleasurscape, debuted at the Rice University Art Gallery in Houston, Texas, in 2001. Rashid conceived the biomorphic interior as a kind of prototype for a future in which objects and spaces will be connected intimately and indistinguishably. It took the form of a series of molded white plastic shapes rising up seamlessly from a continuous floor covering. The undulations in the plastic landscape formed chaise lounges and pedestal-like projections. In his book, he explains the concept:

Pleasurscape sets a stage for a nonstop amorphous plastic scape that denotes a world with no boundaries. The space extends itself via plastic organic modules of repetition—a continuum of surface based

In 1999, Rashid created the winning design for Consolidated Edison's Commemorative Millennium Manhole Cover. Working in the virtual design space of his computer, Rashid "morphed, bulged, and mutated" a Manhattan street grid into a stylized, globe-shaped pattern, which became the 32-inch (81cm) -wide, 314-pound (142kg), cast iron cover.

Rashid re-imagined the bulging grid pattern from his millennium manhole cover for the face of his OP Pocket Watch.

Rashid stretched his amoeboid aesthetic beyond individual objects with an art installation, a 400-square-foot (122 square-meter), biomorphic interior called Pleasurscape, which debuted at the Rice University Art Gallery in Houston, Texas, in 2001.

on the conventional Cartesian grid of the gallery floor. Pleasurscape is a metaphor for a continuous world, a neutral landscape, and an undulating surface that is reconfigurable and extendable ad infinitum.

The 400-square-foot (122 square-meter) installation was made from three modules that could be assembled in various arrangements, resulting in "an extension of the natural landscape to the artificial landscape."

Softscape, a very similar interior landscape concept, debuted as another art installation that same year at San Francisco's Museum of Modern Art, at a show called "010101: Art in Technological Times." Softscape was designed to be literally softer than its hard-plastic predecessor, with the added feature of embedded technology (television, music, telecommunications, etc). With this design, Rashid began to articulate his vision of "infosthetics," the aesthetics of the information age. Of his computer-generated, "completely biomorphic" landscape, Rashid wrote: "The notion is a small, abstract **blobscape** that suggests or alludes to an infinite reconfigurable system for personal configurations…. The soft interior landscape provides all the necessary postures and anthropometrics for a more pleasurable and comfortable life…."

That same year, Rashid collaborated with the principals at Asymptote Architects—his brother, Hani Rashid, and his wife and partner, Lise Ann Couture—to create yet another interior bioform landscape installation. Commissioned by the Institute of Contemporary Art in New York, Stratascape Asymptote comprised a charcoal-gray landscape of Karim-designed reclining chairs, beds, and tables, matched with a suspension of irregularly shaped tubes of molded Plexiglas made by Asymptote. Bubbled images were projected onto the Plexiglas surfaces, making the structure seem to be changing constantly with the swirl and colors of differing patterns.

In 2002, Rashid took his vision of an interior landscape in a somewhat more practical direction with a modular seating system he called Surface Scape. Created for Edra, Rashid's rearrangeable seating scheme featured foam construction, raw-cut edges, and flowing silhouettes. The multicolored interior furniture system was covered with colorful fabric in patterns reminiscent of the sixties and seventies. It comprised four units—chaise/seat, multilevel seat, carpet/seat, and booth/couch—that could be arranged in a variety of ways.

This rolling, biomorphic interior landscape has been described as a "visionary lounge environment" and "anti-conventional seating." Edra called the systems a "carpet-cum-sofa, giving the possibility of an eastern kind of relaxation, whilst guaranteeing the ergonomic support of a modern sofa," and billed as "a master plan for modern living."

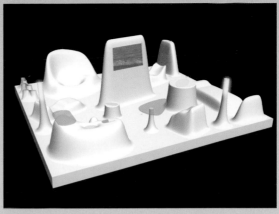

Softscape, which was very similar in concept to Pleasurscape, debuted as another art installation in 2001 at San Francisco's Museum of Modern Art. Rashid designed it to be literally softer than its hard-plastic predecessor, with the added feature of embedded technology (television, music, telecommunications, etc).

With the technology available to devise and reproduce, quickly and cheaply, virtually any conceivable bump, wrinkle, or fold, the forms of many modern devices, particularly consumer electronics, assumed a distinctly organic quality during the 1990s and early 2000s. The amoebic contours of a generation of desktop computers, PDAs, cell phones, and CD players earned these objects, for better or worse, a new label: **blobject**.

The name coined by designer Karim Rashid for his famous couch is now a part of the popular lexicon. Virtually any rounded gadget made of plastic, from the Oral B toothbrush to Logitech's MX 700 Cordless Mouse, has been called a "**blobject**." The word has yet to make its way into mainstream dictionaries, but definitions may be found in a range of zeitgeist-driven publications and on edgy websites. Paul McFedries's Word Spy website defines it as "An object with a curvilinear, flowing design, such as the Apple iMac computer and the Volkswagen Beetle." The British newsletter, *Plain English*, in its "Jargon Buster" column, defined it as "something that has a curved design such as a Volkswagen Beetle." It was one of the American Dialect Society's Words of the Year in 2003; that group called it "a product like the iMac with curvilinear design." In his funny and insightful essay, "**Blobjects** & Biodesign," science fiction writer and technology critic Bruce Sterling offered the single most succinct characterization of **blobjects**: he called them "blown goo." He also mentioned the "humpy, perky, retro-moderne New Beetle" as an example of the form.

Indeed, the New Beetle and the iMac are probably the two most commonly cited examples of **blobjects**, although their designers would doubtless reject that tag. Both machines debuted in the same year, and both are widely considered to be design milestones.

The people's car
Developed in the 1930s, the "humpy" Volkswagen Beetle is one of the most widely recognized silhouettes in the world, and a certified pop culture icon. In his book, *Bug: The Strange Mutations of the World's Most Famous Automobile* (Simon & Schuster, 2002), author Phil Patton characterized the Beetle as "a shape, a set of ideas, and a selfish meme." (A "meme" is an information pattern that propagates itself among human minds—catch phrases, tunes, fashion, ways of making pots—much as genes propagate themselves in the gene pool.)

Credit for the original Beetle concept generally goes to Adolph Hitler, who, during his first year as Chancellor of Germany, spoke often and publicly of his desire for a mass-produced "people's car"—in German, a volkswagen. He is said to have met with the great racecar engineer Ferdinand Porsche at a Berlin auto show in 1933 to discuss his ideas. Hitler reportedly told

chapter 8

outside the beige box
Device designers shake hands with the **blob**

The shape of the original line of Volkswagen Beetles, developed in Germany during the 1930s, had much more to do with the latest theories of aerodynamics than with any desire to impart the vehicle with an organic form factor.

The VW Beetle made its way to the U.S. in about 1955, and the humpy little car enjoyed popularity as a counterculture icon throughout the 1960s and 1970s. A VW ad from the period declared that the Beetle and the Coke bottle were the two best known shapes in the world.

Porsche, "It should look like a beetle; you've only got to look to nature to find out what streamlining is."

The insect reference notwithstanding, the shape of the original line of Beetles had much more to do with the latest theories of aerodynamics than with any desire to impart the vehicle with an organic form factor. The idea of applying concepts from aircraft engineering to the design of automobiles was being explored at the time by Carl Breer, chief engineer at Chrysler. Breer studied vehicle body shapes in wind tunnel tests, believing that by reversing the curves of an airplane wing and applying them to an earthbound vehicle, he could create a counter-lift effect that would give cars a more secure hold on the road at high speeds and a generally steadier ride. The result of Breer's research was the Chrysler Airflow, which featured a sharply sloped nose and headlights and fenders that were smoothed into the car's body. It looked a lot like the highly successful PT Cruiser, which Chrysler launched in the 2002 model year.

Natural forms still seem to have had some influence on the car's design, at least in the minds of the writers in the Chrysler public relations department. In an advertisement for the Airflow that appeared in a 1934 issue of Fortune magazine, the company declared:

You have only to look at a dolphin, a gull, or a greyhound to appreciate the rightness of the tapering, flowing contour of the new Airflow Chrysler. By scientific experiment, Chrysler engineers have simply verified and adapted a natural fundamental law.

Some historians report that Porsche wanted to develop a German version of the streamlined Tatra T87. The Czech vehicle looked something like a comic-book spaceship with a kind of dorsal fin running down its back. But Porsche is also thought to have studied the Airflow when he visited the U.S. in 1936 to research technology for his Volkswagen prototype. The influence of the American vehicle can be see in the first Beetles, which were called KdF-wagens, for Kraft durch Freude ("power by joy").

The Beetle made its way to the U.S. in about 1955. Throughout the 1960s and 1970s, the "Bug" enjoyed popularity as a counterculture icon—thanks to American marketing know-how. A VW ad in the 60s declared that the Beetle and the Coke bottle were the two best known shapes in the world. Walt Disney anthropomorphized the vehicle to create the *Herbie, the Love Bug* film series. The Beetle would eventually become the best selling car of all time, with over 20 million sold worldwide.

During the 1980s, the car's popularity waned and Volkswagen's fortunes declined in the face of better-designed cars from Japan. In the 1990s, the company sought to recapture market share by re-imagining their iconic auto with a modern version they called the New Beetle.

The car's key designer was J.C. Mays, then working in VW's Simi Valley, California, studio. According to one story, Mays was eating sushi with another VW designer, Peter Schreyer in 1991, discussing Volkswagen's then lackluster performance in the U.S., when he hit upon the idea of reviving the Beetle. Another story holds that Volkswagen approached its Simi Valley team in 1993 to come up with a concept car to commemorate the Beetle in an upcoming auto show. Wherever the idea came from, Mays worked with another VW designer, Freeman Thomas, to create the prototype of the New Beetle, which received rave reviews when it debuted in 1994 as

an auto-show concept car.

The final production version of the car—its fifth iteration—was unveiled at the 1998 Detroit Auto Show. The vehicle's design reflected the form of its progenitor, combined with modern automotive technologies and features. And it was distinctly more biomorphic; the line of its arc-shaped roof incorporated the windshield, the rear window, and the trunk lid, creating a single, smooth curve. The bulge of the hood was bluntly rounded. And its deep-draw, injection-molded, NORYL GTX resin fenders swelled slightly, like flexed shoulders.

Mays conceptualized his efforts on the project with the phrase "progressive emotional optimism," which he said was an approach to design that respects history while embracing technology and simplified forms. Some have called the project a "deliberate reinterpretation" of the legendary car. Others have seen it as a calculated stab at the nostalgic vein of aging baby boomers who associated the Bug with the good old days. For Mays, the project was as much about re-creating a cultural symbol as it was about building an automobile. "Pop culture is the only culture we have left," Mays said in an interview, "...As much as [the Beetle] is an icon, it is also a huge piece of our pop culture."

Volkswagen had been losing market share for years when the company decided to create a re-imagined version of its iconic auto for a 1994 auto show. The concept car's key designer was J.C. Mays, then working in VW's Simi Valley, California, studio. Mays worked with another VW designer, Freeman Thomas, to create the prototype of the New Beetle, which received rave reviews at the show and then sold like hotcakes when it hit the car dealerships in 1998.

Apple wowed the computer world in 1998
with a radical rethink of the PC form factor.
In place of the blinking beige boxes that had
stood monolithically on our desktops for
more than a decade, Apple offered an
organically rounded, translucently colorful
blobject: the iMac.

Thinking different

Steve Jobs and Steve Wozniak founded Apple Computer in the late 1970s and launched the personal computer revolution from a Silicon Valley garage. The company introduced the Macintosh in 1984, a PC that revolutionized the revolution with innovations like the mouse and the point-and-click graphical user interface. And in 1998, Apple wowed the world again with a radical rethinking of the PC form factor. In place of the blinking beige boxes that had stood monolithically on our desktops for more than a decade, Apple offered an organically rounded, translucently colorful **blobject**: the iMac.

No design has shaken up the computer world quite like the fashion-forward face and form of Apple's iMac. Apple CEO Steve Jobs reportedly told the company's chief designer, British-born Jonathan Ive, to build "George Jetson's computer." Ive and his design team took that glib directive as a mandate to take some risks, and the design they came up with was the aesthetic antithesis of everything else on the market.

"The sad thing was that many people were missing out on this immensely powerful machine—the computer—because they were so terrified," Ives told the British *Daily Telegraph*. "It's been thrilling to see how people relate to this simple device. The talk is not about speed or memory but what you can do with it."

Some aspects of the new machine were reminiscent of the "classic" Mac of 1984; it was a cute, simple, all-in-one PC with a handle that made it "luggable." But in most ways, it was brand spanking new. The iMac wasn't a box, but a fleshy bulge, and instead of geek-orthodox beige, it was "bondi" blue and white, with interesting surface textures, and ports and slots worked into clever curves. Its curvilinear form was mirrored by its round, semi-transparent mouse, which had a two-tone ball.

A year after the bondi blue iMac hit the shelves, Apple released the machine in five new colors, including blueberry (aquamarine), strawberry (pinkish-red), tangerine (orangish-yellow), lime (bright green), and grape (purple). Later, the company added indigo (dark blue), ruby (candy apple red), sage (gray-green), graphite (gray), and snow (white). Apple also offered two limited-edition color schemes: Blue Dalmatian (royal blue with baby blue spots), and Flower Power (a multicolored, "1960's-era youth culture inspired" flower pattern).

Associated Press writer Chris Allbritton credited Ive's take on the PC with launching an industrial design trend. "Apple's designs, envisioned by Jonathon Ive…have not only changed the look of computing," he wrote, "but spilled out into the rest of society, almost single-handedly starting the '**blobject**' craze for curvy, organic items."

Ive, who went on to create the unique look of the G4, the iBook, the Cube, and the iPod, has said that his design team's goals for the original iMacs weren't merely aesthetic. "With the first iMac the goal wasn't to look different, but to build the best integrated consumer computer we could," Ives said in an interview. "If as a consequence the shape is different, then that's how it is. The thing is, it's very easy to be different, but very difficult to be better. That's what we have tried to do with the new iMac."

When the machine debuted, it was both praised and derided by industry watchers. In some design circles, it was considered a classic and a popular design milestone. "The iMac begins the process of exploring how a computer might be something other than just a keyboard and a TV," Stanford University design professor Barry Katz told *Wired* magazine's Joe Nickell. "It's exploring the envelope." Writing in the Sunday edition of the British *Observer*, Jim McClellan called the iMac "...the high-water mark of the so-called **'blobject'** design aesthetic…." IDEO's Bill Moggridge saw the iMacs as examples of a "personalistic" approach. "These kinds of designs use strong colors and distinctive shapes," he explains. "They shout, so to speak. They say, I'm telling a big, strong story. I'm bold! I'm a simple form! I'm brightly colored! I'm here!"

Some critics saw the new form-factor changes as trivial and superficial. They seemed to find it hard to take seriously a **blobby** computer that came in candy colors. It looked like a "beach ball," a "goldfish bowl," an "alien chicken egg"; it was "the New Beetle of PCs." Some industry wags even called it the "**iBlob**."

But the simple fact was, its technological and performance improvements notwithstanding—and there were many—the iMacs made other PCs look drab and boring by comparison. Consumers responded to its striking industrial design, and the machine sold like hotcakes—more than 400,000 units in its first month on the market, according to Apple; 2 million units in the first year.

In an interview conducted for Apple with Delphine Hirasuna, Ive argued that product differentiation should not be a designer's first goal, and he insisted that it was not his as he designed the iMac. "I think a lot of people see design primarily as a means to differentiate their product competitively," he said. "I really detest that. That is just a corporate agenda, not a customer or people agenda. It is important to understand that our goal wasn't just to differentiate our product, but to create products that people would love in the future. Differentiation was a consequence of our goal."

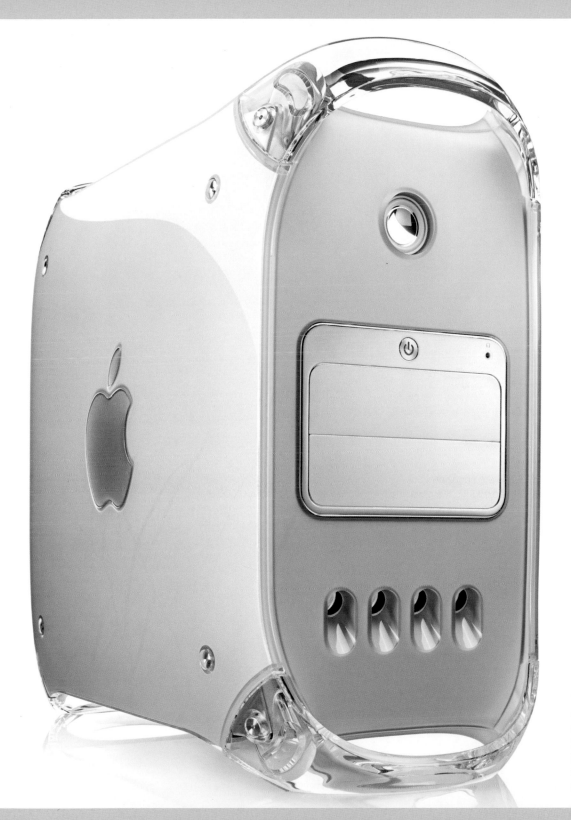

The iMac's designer, Jonathan Ive, went on to create the unique look of the G4, the iBook, the Cube, and the iPod. He has said that his design team's goals for the original iMacs weren't merely aesthetic, but "to build the best integrated consumer computer we could."

IDEO's slim, curvilinear design of the Palm V personal digital assistant was a genuine trend setter. Half as thick as its predecessor, with a thin-yet-rigid anodized aluminum skin, it was a wide departure from what had come before it.

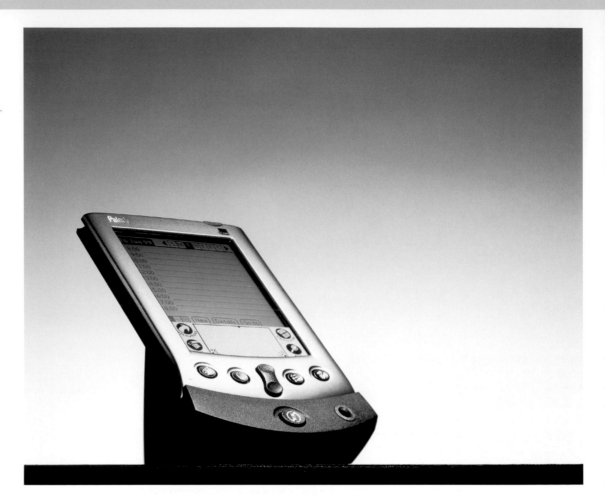

Is that a blob in your hand?

Even before the **blobby** iMac shook up the PC world with its radical design, some high-tech manufacturers were seriously rethinking the looks of their products. The cell phone industry in particular was leading the trend, trimming and softening its phones with organic curves. The thin, ultralight, nearly angle-free design of the Motorola StarTac, which debuted in 1996, had made the slim, black cell phone into a genuine status symbol in business circles. It was selling for around $1,000, even at a time when wireless service providers were giving cell phones away.

Dennis Boyle, a studio leader and principal of the IDEO industrial design firm, believes that aesthetic considerations become more important as our devices "mature." In a 2002 interview with *NewsFactor*'s Marsha Zager, he pointed to the evolution of automobiles and airplanes, which began as unadorned machinery, but later became dazzling, highly designed objects of desire. "They start out with people just trying to make them work," Boyle told Zager. "But eventually people don't care what's inside."

This principle is particularly evident in the evolution of personal electronics, from wristwatches to personal digital assistants (PDAs). "If you carry it with you around the clock, you want it to add to your style, like clothing or jewelry or accessories," Boyle told Zager. "You don't want people to say it looks nerdy or geeky." Indeed, the StarTac, with its spare, plastic holster, was wearable.

Boyle, who would later design the Handspring Treo PDA and work on a range of computing devices for Apple, Dell, and Hewlett-Packard, led the project team that designed one of the best examples of this principle in action: the Palm V.

Unveiled in 1996, the original PalmPilot PDA was the first hand-held, pen-based computing device to succeed in the marketplace since the premature death of Apple's before-its-time Newton in 1998. Early technology adopters, mostly men, loved it, and it quickly became the fastest-selling computer product ever. But early versions of the device were boxy and not much more aesthetically interesting than their big, beige brothers on the desktop. As competitors began crowding the newly opened market for PDAs, Palm reached out to IDEO for a design with wider appeal.

IDEO is probably the largest and certainly among the most innovative product design firms in the world. It is responsible for some striking and innovative product designs. Co-founder David Kelley designed Apple's first mouse in 1982. The firm is responsible for Polaroid's I-Zone instant camera, the Softbook digital reader, and the Steelcase Leapchair. In 1999, ABC News filmed a documentary of the firm in action, tackling ABC's challenge to redesign a shopping cart in five working days. (That show later aired on Nightline.)

Based in Palo Alto, California, in the heart of Silicon Valley, IDEO was well known at the time as a highly creative, technologically sophisticated operation. It seemed the perfect choice to reposition the next-generation Palm using design to set it apart from its many imitators and establish the device as a desirable accessory. IDEO's Boyle reportedly brought a StarTac to his first meeting with Palm creator Jay Hawkins. Hawkins told Boyle that he wanted a design with the same visceral impact.

The Palm project was code-named "Razor," leaving no doubt about at least one design goal: make the device thinner. Boyle distributed dozens of PalmPilots to colleagues and friends. More than 200 staffers within the firm began using the PDAs. Gathering feedback from these product testers, he paid special attention to the comments of female users. Most liked the device very much, but all agreed that it was too fat, too heavy, and too square. And the stylus storage was a pain. The women in particular wanted a sleeker device with softer edges and some color other than gray.

The project took three years and continued through several management changes at Palm. Just before the project started Palm Computing had been bought by U.S. Robotics, which turned around and sold the company to 3Com, which a few years later would spin off Palm into its own company through an initial public offering. Palm Computing's founder, Jay Hawkins, would leave 3Com to start Handspring, a PDA maker that would license the Palm operating system.

The final design cut the thickness of the old model in half by replacing the Palm's AAA batteries with a rechargeable lithium ion power source. Curves were added, and the thick plastic hide was replaced with a thin-yet-rigid anodized aluminum skin. To eliminate bulky screws, IDEO used industrial glue to hold the device together. The design included integrated side rails that could serve as stylus storage, to attach a leather cover flap, and/or secure the device in third-party covers and cases.

The Palm V was striking. Its design was such a wide departure from what had come before that it both set the device apart from its current competitors and established a new, more organic form-factor standard for PDAs and hand-helds. Early advertisements for the Palm V emphasized its organic qualities and the idea that such a device could be fashionable. Portrait photographer Timothy Greenfield-Sanders, whose work had appeared in such publications as *Vanity Fair* and *Vogue*, shot the sleek little PDA resting in the hand of a naked female dancer, kneeling with her arms and legs folded around her. The caption read: "Simply Palm." The ad ran in magazines and on billboards, and it sparked controversy when critics labeled it sexist. In its response to one critic, Palm wrote:

The female image in the advertisement was designed to draw a parallel between the elegant design of the Palm V organizer and the elegance of the human form. We wanted to show that great design involves both the aesthetics of an element as well as how that element functions or performs. In the case of the dancer's image, the human form is the backdrop to the Palm V organizer and not the focus of the ad. The simplicity of the imagery and the

"Simply Palm" headline are meant to reflect the simplicity that is the cornerstone of our product design philosophy and a key factor in our success.

Palm eventually published a version of the ad with a male model, but soon switched to less incendiary imagery.

The blob as postmodern rejoinder
The New Beetle, the first iMacs, and the Palm V are examples of an industrial design drift toward eye-catching curves and organic form factors. But their digitally adept creators weren't the first industrial designers to express an organic aesthetic. For IDEO co-founder Bill Moggridge, **blobism** fits neatly into the larger landscape of post-modernism.

Designers such as Ettore Sottsass and George Sowden, who came together in 1981 to form the Memphis design group, weren't **blobist**, but their work displayed a particularly rebellious quality. The group's stable of designers included

Michele de Lucchi, Andrea Branzi, and Michael Graves. Their primary goal was to revive Radical Design, and their work all but exploded with bright colors, bold patterns, and materials the design world had not seen before. They employed neon, exotic veneers, and wildly patterned plastic laminates to break with conventional forms and poke fun at the seriousness of functional designs. Their work evolved into a style that would come to define 1980s design.

"The materials tell this story about being allowed to suddenly use decorative elements," Moggridge explains. "The designs were new, strong, different, very anti-strict-modernism. Sottsass's work is particularly beautiful when he combines these rather brash ideas that push color and shape with very traditional materials, such as glass, where the craftsmanship adds an incredible sense of quality. It's something that's new and fresh but has traditional value."

Superstar designer Philippe Starck might well be seen as another significant link in the postmodern-to-**blob** chain. His organic impulses can be seen in his spiderlike Lemon Squeezer.

The smooth curves and muscular contours of Starck's Lama Scooter, although not precisely **blobist**, are certainly drawn from natural forms.

Starck's Barstool design evinces the form of a jellyfish.

The Austrian-born Sottsass was the acknowledged leader of the Anti-Design movement, which opposed the "correct" and "good taste" of functionalism. Sottsass wanted to break down the barriers between high-class and low-class design. He is known for his experiments with the new material fiberglass, which he used to develop contemporary furniture and lighting. As a consultant to the Olivetti company, he designed adding machines, computers, and furniture. His Olivetti Valentine typewriter was a cherry-red portable plastic machine that broke dramatically from office equipment design convention.

Interestingly, Sowden was an early adopter of the digital tools of his trade. After the Memphis group disbanded in 1988, he formed Studio Sowden to pursue his growing interest in the interaction between design and computer technology. When Davy Kho, Hiroshi Ono, and Franco Mele joined the group in 1994, it became Milan-Pacific. Collaboration was key for Sowden, and his group eventually developed a new digital paradigm for the design process that allowed for increased interactions among designers. "The speed at which we process information creates energy around the project," Sowden explained in an interview, "[it] conveys the idea of pleasure in creating and makes space to involve other people in the development."

Moggridge points to superstar French designer Phillippe Starck as another significant link in this post-modern-to-**blob** chain. Starck is one of the best known, brand-name designers in the world. He has designed kitchen appliances, tooth-brushes, office furniture, vehicles, computers, doorknobs, glasses frames, lamps, boats, and mineral-water bottles.

Starck's subversive, intelligent and always interesting approach to design hardly makes him a **blobist**, but he clearly has found inspiration for many of his industrial designs in natural forms. Examples abound: his spiderlike Lemon Squeezer, his curvilinear Lama Scooter, barstools that look like jellyfish, a Recyclable Television set that appears to be housed in a walnut shell.

"You can see this sort of taking the inspiration of the organic forms of nature and making products that are really driven and derived from that," Moggridge says. "You find lots of examples of [Starck's] work, both in architectural interiors and products, that are very much driven by this new way of looking at shapes that come from natural forms."

Design dissolving into behavior
Industrial design may be drifting back to a new rationalism, flirting with the original values of modernism, particularly in the case of digital devices. On the other side of **blobism**, Moggridge sees the emergence of a trend he calls

"design dissolving into behavior."

"If you look at Apple's newest products, for example," Moggridge explains, "you see what looks on the aesthetic surface to be a return to modernism. The new devices look more like Dieter Rams than anything has in a while. But if you look closer, you'll see that the excitement has moved from the object itself to the behavior of the software. What is happening on the screen has become very rich—bright colors, sounds, animation. But the object has become much more set back in order to be a stage for that behavior."

Compare, for example, IDEO's trend-setting design of the Palm V, with its more recent design of the Handspring Visor Edge. IDEO was hired to provide industrial design and mechanical engineering for the Visor Edge, and to create a "form that enhances the Visor line while defining a visual identity distinct from other handheld devices." The firm that had given organic curves to the Palm V so that it would stand out among its boxy competitors would soon be putting corners on the Visor Edge to differentiate it from a pack of **blobjects**.

Both PDAs are thin and metal-cased, but the forms of the two devices differ markedly. Where the Palm is organic and curvilinear, the Visor Edge is crisply angular. The Handspring device's anodized aluminum housing came in three colors, and it came with a removable hinged metal cover to protect the display. The soft-sculpted, die-cast zinc stylus (with a plastic writing tip) contrasted with Visor Edge's clean, rectilinear lines. And with a thickness of $7/16$ of an inch (7mm), the Visor Edge out-razored the Razor. "It has a delicate elegance," Moggridge says. "It's quieter. It feels very laid back and gentle compared with something like the [original] iMac. The excitement is in what you can do with it. This is what I think of as **post-blobitecture**."

IDEO also designed the Visor Edge to accept the detachable Springboard slot, a minimal "backpack" that mounts on the top edge of the device, and accepts a variety of Springboard accessories, such as a digital camera, a cell phone, or a GPS receiver.

"People associate design often with individuals," Moggridge adds.

"But you can't do the sophisticated stuff with just one guy. If you've got something that has behavioral qualities about it, you have to design the software, the service, the environment, the brand—lots of things besides the object. And individuals just can't do that. So you need an integrated, creative team. IDEO is divided into interdisciplinary studios, kept small and intimate enough so that they feel like the people can do exciting work together. If you get too big, they feel like they're in a factory, and that just kills that sense of creativity."

On the other side of **blobism**, designs such as IDEO's sleek Visor Edge PDA may augur a return to the angles and edges of earlier design values—what IDEO's Bill Moggridge calls "design dissolving into behavior," a trend in which the focus is on what's happening on the device's screen.

A number of IDEO design teams worked on Visor Edge, including an industrial design group, a manufacturing engineering group, a mechanical engineering group, and a group to design the "human factors."

Quintessence of computational coolness

Released in 2002, Apple's Titanium PowerBook G4 laptop computers seem to be a particularly apt example of Morrgridge's idea. A one-inch (3cm) -thick, silvery slab when closed, the Titanium is lean and angular, displaying what *ID* magazine called "control and restraint." With a titanium "skin" stretched over a carbon-fiber frame, the machine was light, durable, and understated.

The second generation of iMacs fit the model, too. The first machines were designed around tube-based CRT monitors—basically, TV screens. The new version unveiled at the 2002 Macworld Expo incorporated a flat, liquid-crystal display into an utterly unique stem-and-base design.

It took Apple about two years to design and develop the new iMac, unofficially dubbed the "Flat-Panel iMac" by EveryMac.com. After the decision was made to switch from a CRT to an LCD, it fell to Jonathan Ive and his design team to come up with Apple's first "flat" PC. Early approaches involved mounting components right behind the display, essentially in the space previously occupied by the cathode ray tube. But there was nothing flat about the results. This configuration also limited screen mobility, and it required vertical mounting of the computer's disc drives, which would make them run slower than a traditional horizontal orientation.

Eventually, inspired by the sight of a sunflower growing in Steve Jobs's wife's garden, Ive and company hit upon the idea of a "free-floating"

screen mounted on an adjustable "neck," with the components housed in a small-footprint base that would be heavy enough to provide stability. "We had to liberate the display, explode it, disconnect it from the CPU," Ive told the British *Independent News*. Ports would be in the back of the base; expansion slots on the bottom. The stainless-steel neck would swivel 180-degrees around the base, and allow users to change its tilt angle from -5 to 30 degrees.

The neck (sometimes it's called an "articulating arm") not only held up the monitor, but it was so sturdily built that Apple told users to feel free to use it as a handle when they picked up the roughly 22-pound (10kg) machine.

When Jobs took the wraps off the new machine at the Macworld show, he called it "the quintessence of computational coolness," and the crowd agreed. But by then, many had already seen it. *Time* magazine had scooped Jobs, giving the world a pre-conference look at the groundbreaking iMacs in a cover story. It was "like no computer ever seen before," enthused Josh Quittner, the *Time* writer. "…the 15-inch (38cm) LCD screen hangs, seeming to float in the air."

Quittner and many others thought the decidedly less organic new iMac looked like a desk lamp; almost no one seems to have caught the sunflower connection. He also spotted the machine's resemblance to Luxo Jr., the hopping, swing-arm lamp that serves as the logo of animation company Pixar Studios, which Jobs founded in 1986 during his famous hiatus from Apple. A few observers thought the new iMac looked like E.T.

Ironing out the lumps

Even Karim Rashid, a designer whose name is synonymous with

blobism, was seen to add a crease or two to some of his later work. In 1999, Rashid's design of an Issey Miyake 2-in-1 travel kit was markedly square and spare. In 2002, *ID* magazine's annual design awards recognized Rashid's "Escher-esque" bottle and case for Shiseido's 5S Metasense perfume, awarding it Best of Category in packaging design. The jurors were fascinated with the "complex, angular shapes," and even remarked on the design's departure from what they called the "**blobular** packaging so common among avant-garde perfumeries." The blow-molded, translucent-white polypropylene bottle and case "adeptly combine hard and soft in a single packaging aesthetic," *ID* said. "Angular without appearing sharp, the translucent plastic pieces work together to suggest a mysterious and tactile form." Rashid reportedly said that the bottle's unusual five-pointed shape reflected the 5S name.

In a way, Moggridge's notions of design dissolving into behavior apply even here; Rashid told the magazine, "I generally start perfume design by using the smell as a point of entry…I could smell love, peace, synthetics, lambent, organic." The designer bestowed a classic Rashidism on his olefactory interaction with the product. He called it "technorganic," because "the fragrance had an overwhelming, provocative memory of unknown scents mixed with the deepest sense of nature. I believe that experience is completely sensorial, and design must engage all the senses. This is how I approach all my clients and projects."

It should be noted, however, that Rashid's classically **blobby** version of the Issey Miyake Summer Fragrance bottle was also cited in the same 2002 awards for Design Distinction.

The **post-blobist** trend has even manifested in the latest incarnation of quintessential **blob** device. The newest iMac utilizes a flat screen riding on an articulating arm. The inspiration, though, was organic: the sight of a sunflower growing in Apple Computer CEO Steve Jobs's wife's garden.

iMac

next generation

The **post-blobists** get real

It's not surprising, in this fast-paced and ever-accelerating Information Age, that we should already be hearing about a "second generation" of digitally driven designers who are actively questioning and stretching the theories and practices of their discipline. These pragmatic, computer-savvy architects are using technology, not for conceptual design and experimentation, but to develop and support competitive practices that are committed to built work.

This is a group that has taken to heart architect Norman Foster's admonition never to forget that "the silent, invisible electronic world" of virtual design must ultimately end in "physical reality."

These architects also place an emphasis on open models of practice—a model exemplified by SHoP/Sharples Holden Pasquarelli. Indeed, there is perhaps no better example of this new pragmatic generation. "…SHoP represents an entirely new kind of firm," Christopher Hawthorne observed in *Metropolis*, "one riding the crest of architecture's digital wave… [A] couple of decades from now, when all the best-known baby boomers have shuffled off to the cultural periphery, the architecture world may well be left with a whole lot of firms that look, sound, and talk like SHoP."

The New York–based firm was formed in 1996 by twin brothers William and Christopher Sharples; William's wife, Coren Sharples; Kimberly Holden; and Holden's husband, Gregg Pasquarelli (thus, the acronymic "SHoP"). Although the firm utilizes 3-D animation software in some processes that are similar to the **blobist** approach, the five SHoP partners see the technology differently. They have focused on moving beyond what might be thought of as an academic absorption with computer-aided imagery, emphasizing instead the use of digi-

tal techniques to meet design and construction challenges in the real world. They combine 3-D digital design software with rapid prototyping practices and their own in-house model building facilities to generate designs that are both original and buildable. As the firm's press kit puts it, these are no-nonsense designers who "link emerging concepts and theories of the digital age with the tactile fundamentals of design and construction."

"The five of us began having these conversations about what the hell this profession was," Pasquarelli told Hawthorne. "There were no models that interested us. We didn't want to be the daring avant-gardists, the corporate firm, the starving artists, the academics." And he added, "The computer has been a tool that's helped us to develop a new model. It's not about the form." (It is interesting to note that Pasquarelli worked for both Frank Gehry and Greg Lynn.)

Erected at P.S.1's Long Island facility, the 12,000-square-foot (3,700-square-meter) Dunescape structure was made of more than 6,000 2-by-2-inch (5-by-5-centimeter) cedar strips, with a vinyl surface that bent and folded to accommodate various spatial configurations. The designers took the forms of common objects found at the beach—beach chair, umbrella, boogie board, and cabana—and morphed them on the computer into continuously curved, self-structuring surfaces that formed archipelagos of ribbed wooden spaces.

Created in 2000 for an annual series of competitions jointly sponsored by the Museum of Modern Art and the P.S. 1 Contemporary Art Center in Queens, New York, Dunescape was one of SHoP's most attention-getting projects and the program's debut competition winner.

An attitude and an ideology

The SHoP partners coined the term "versioning" for their approach, and they consider it to be an entirely new model for architectural practice. It is a "logic-based" design strategy that encompasses concepts like "value engineering," and coordinates the many variables of design and construction processes into a single computerized system. As new information becomes available or as design requirements change, the data is fed into the system. Versioning takes advantage of the computer's ability to "change design processes in the act of making," to "expand, in time as well as in territory, the potential effects of design." According to the firm, versioning can be seen as an attitude rather than an ideology:

[Versioning] allows architects to think or practice across multiple disciplines, freely borrowing tactics from film, food, finance, fashion, economics, and politics for use in design, or reversing the model and using architectural theory to participate in other problem solving fields. Versioning is important to architects because it attempts to remove architecture from a stylistically driven cycle of consumption.

Versioning is also meant to describe what the SHoP architects perceive to be a shift in the roles of architects and designers, largely facilitated by computer technology. Traditionally responsible for little more than the generation of plans and images, they perceive, and practice, a more vertically integrated approach to the discipline. They describe it this way:

The computer has enabled architects to rethink the design process in terms of procedure and outcome in ways that common practice, the construction industry, and conventional design methodologies cannot conceive of. This, in turn, has had an equally profound impact on legal practices, insurance liabilities, and design/production partnerships, thereby initiating a restructuring of the traditional relations of power, responsibility, and accountability in design.

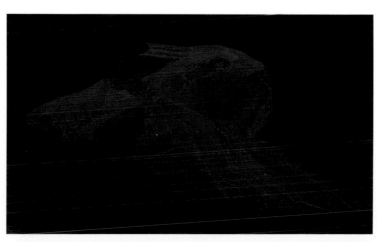

The five SHoP partners utilize computer design software in some processes that are similar to the **blobist** approach (their design of Dunescape, for example, rendered here). But the SHoP architects focus on moving beyond what might be thought of as an academic absorption with computer-aided imagery, emphasizing instead the use of digital techniques to meet design and construction challenges in the real world.

As of this writing, SHoP has designed a range of projects, including a university academic building, a civic park, two public art installations, a museum, retail shops, and two mid-rise apartment buildings.

The anti-blob
One of the firm's most attention-getting projects was created in 2000 for an annual series of competitions jointly sponsored by the Museum of Modern Art and the P.S. 1 Contemporary Art Center in Queens, New York. SHoP designed the program's debut competition winner, a temporary pavilion conceived as "a day at the shore," and called Dunescape.

Erected at P.S. 1's Long Island facility, the 12,000-square-foot (3,700-square-meter) structure was made of more than 6,000 2-by-2-inch cedar strips, with a vinyl surface that bent and folded to accommodate various spatial configurations. The designers took the forms of common objects found at the beach—beach chair, umbrella, boogie board, and cabana—and morphed them on the computer into continuously curved, self-structuring surfaces that formed archipelagos of ribbed wooden spaces, what *Washington Post* writer Benjamin Forgey called a "splendid, slithering structure." The long structure formed itself into sun decks, chaises,

changing rooms, awnings, and wading pools with its swerving surfaces.

The firm explains the shifting roles of the structure's surfaces this way:

When the surface is high in the air, it provides shade, when it is lower it provides inclined seating areas. When it is on its side, it becomes a thickened translucent wall, creating individual "cabanas" where visitors may change their clothing. As it twists onto the ground "lifeguard" stands also serve as "dancing" platforms. Water runs along the entire surface collecting in pools throughout the courtyard where the surface touches the ground. A mist garden disperses water throughout the air.

"SHoP's interactive forms invite sunning, sitting, wading, drinking, cruising," *New York Magazine*'s Joseph Giovannini wrote of the project. "The forms precipitate the situation and sculpt the event." *New Yorker* architecture critic, Paul Goldberger, called Dunescape "one of the few instances of computer-enhanced design in which the result is warmer, livelier, and more exciting than the renderings that preceded it."

Although the overall form curves and undulates, it should be noted that there were virtually no curved components in Dunescape; small

pieces and incremental steps created the appearance of continuously curved edges and planes. "It could not have been designed without the computer," Foley declared, "but it appears strangely hand-crafted—in a way, it is an **anti-blob**."

Bridging a gap at ground zero
Nowhere is this new generation's combination of vision and pragmatism better expressed than in SHoP's approach to the design of Lower Manhattan's Rector Street Pedestrian Bridge. Completed in 2002, the bridge is a temporary structure that reconnected the residents and businesses of Battery Park City, which had been isolated by the collapse of the World Trade Center, with the rest of downtown. Battery Park comprises residential neighborhoods, the World Financial Center, and a range of cultural institutions. Prior to the September 11th attack, the area had been linked to the rest of Lower Manhattan by two pedestrian bridges. One was damaged and the other destroyed in the disaster.

The project called for a means of safe passage for up to 4,000 people per hour across West Street, a heavy-traffic corridor fed from the Brooklyn Battery Tunnel. Although the bridge would need to provide shelter from

Nowhere is this new generation of architects' combination of vision and pragmatism better expressed than in SHoP's approach to the design of Lower Manhattan's Rector Street Pedestrian Bridge. Completed in 2002, the bridge is a temporary structure that reconnected the residents and businesses of Battery Park City, which had been isolated by the collapse of the World Trade Center, with the rest of downtown.

weather, no one wanted a dark tube. The design brief called for a structure that would offer occasional views of the surrounding areas.

The need to reconnect these isolated neighborhoods put pressure on the SHoP architects to come up with a solution quickly. They pushed for "a complex form, but a simple solution," and decided on a prefabricated galvanized steel box truss system for the bridge's superstructure, which was supplied by Mabey Bridge.

The designers incorporated a steel roof truss system, mounted to this superstructure, to allow for a roof and partial cladding of the exterior wall surfaces. The perforated cladding would allow light into the bridge during the day, and fluorescent light to emanate at night from five-foot (1.5-meter) long "light planks" set in the floor.

Erected directly south of Ground Zero, the bridge was the first building project of any size to be completed in the area since 9/11. It was commissioned by the Battery Park City Authority (BPCA) within weeks of the attack, and funded by FEMA (Federal Emergency Management Agency). The project itself was a collaborative effort; SHoP worked with Buro Happold consulting engi-

neers, the Battery Park City Authority, the New York State Department of Transportation, and the Sam Schwartz Company.

The location was chosen to provide residents of Battery Park and commuters from the financial center with access to the Rector Street subway stop, the closest subway access to the area. But residents worried that the bridge would cut across the area's few green spaces. Consequently, the structure's orientation was shifted in the final design. "The bridge is on a skew because the community brought their fifth-graders out to the community board meeting and said, 'You can't destroy our only green space,'" Bill Sharples told *Metropolis* writer Jonathan Ringen. "And you know what? Greg [Pasquarelli] and I were convinced."

Camera obscura
Camera Obscura offers one of SHoP's most whimsical designs. A camera obscura (Latin for "dark chamber") is a dark box or room punctured by a tiny hole that shines a bit of light on the opposite side. If the hole is small enough, it projects an inverted image in color of the world outside. These devices have been around for hundreds of years, and the

SHoP architects used the concept as the basis for one of four buildings they designed for a four-acre waterfront park project commissioned by the Village of Greenport, New York. When completed, Mitchell Park will include a glass pavilion for an antique carousel, an outdoor refrigerated ice skating rink that converts to a sprinkler plaza in the summer, and an outdoor amphitheater. According to a report from Greenport, the Camera Obscura would provide "a unique visual perspective of the village and harbor."

The building was conceived of as a camera: A lens admits the exterior light into the 300-square-foot (91-square-meter) building, projecting an upside-down, live image of the surrounding area onto a mirror, which inverts and reflects that image onto a flat, circular table. The table may be raised or lowered to focus the image. The building is located strategically in the park so that the lens may be focused on all of the buildings and grounds, on the nearby marina and even across the bay to Shelter Island.

The SHoP architects created the design for the building using 3-D computer modeling software, and it emerged as a kind of kit of custom parts accompanied by assembly

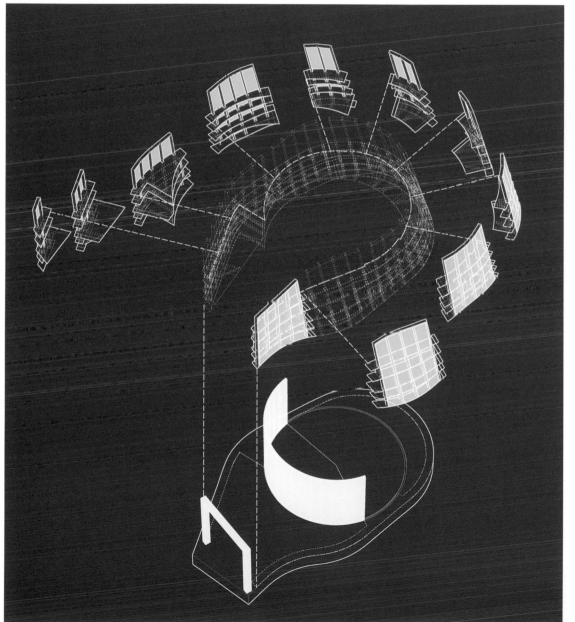

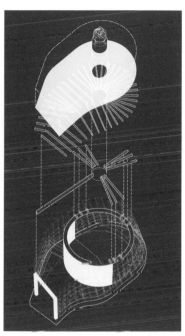

SHoP's whimsical Camera Obscura, one of several buildings commissioned by the Village of Greenport, New York, was created using 3-D computer modeling software as a kind of kit of custom parts accompanied by assembly instructions—something like a model airplane kit. Manufacturers would be able to feed the digital files into computer-enabled fabrication equipment and easily and precisely laser-cut the main aluminum and steel components of the structure.

instructions—something like a model airplane kit. This approach is characteristic of SHoP thinking: Manufacturers would be able to feed the digital files into computer-enabled fabrication equipment, and easily and precisely laser-cut the main aluminum and steel components of the structure. The firm would also provide full-scale templates for wall and roof sheathing, which would be made from a black, paper-resin board called Skatelite, known for its flexibility and widely used in skateboard parks. The structure's pre-fabricated panels would be brought to the site and bolted into the concrete foundation and to each other; the rest of the building's structural elements would be attached to this foundational assembly. The curvilinear exterior skin of the building would be composed of milled ipe hardwood planks, an approach reminiscent of Dunescape.

A resilient and ambiguous correlation

SHoP's approach to its proposed design for the Museum of Sex in Midtown Manhattan was highly conceptual, yet profoundly practical. And it is one of the firm's most blatantly biomorphic designs.

Billed as the first the U.S. museum to preserve and present the history of sex, the 40,000-square-foot (12,200-square-meter) project was planned for a narrow, L-shaped corner in New York City, a site with views of the Empire State Building. The firm conceptualized the unique challenge of designing a museum of human sexuality with a series of questions:

Is there a relationship between form and performance that could aid in the design of a space for human sexuality? A relationship that does not utilize a bifurcating model of male/female, straight/gay, specta-

tor/participant, but a resilient and ambiguous correlation between desires and an architecture that allows a museum of sex to reevaluate ideas and concepts? How would we use the body, form, position, fluidity, tracing, figure, presence, and space to provide a solution for our clients where a symbiosis between a cultural institution and an economic engine, display and consumption, program and event and thought and process will emerge? Imagine how this will expand into fashion, food, culture, and play?

Inspired by the contours of the human body, the firm would design a structural "skin" that would encase the building in translucent layers that peeled back in places to allow vertical movement, light filtration, or to house displays. As the firm explained it, the site's constricted floor plan suggested "a layered

SHoP's approach to its proposed design for the Museum of Sex in Midtown Manhattan was highly conceptual, yet profoundly practical. The 40,000-square-foot (12,200-square-meter) project was planned for a narrow, L-shaped corner in New York City, a site with views of the Empire State Building.

organizational device" which evolved from "the generative concepts of organic form, tactile expression, exposure and concealment." This building's skin would form an "undulating topography composed of layered surfaces with specific functions." The facade would become "part of a flirtatious game played between the building and the city." The result was a striking edifice veiled in luminous planes of glass.

The SHoP's innovative concept for the Museum of Sex was shelved, but the Museum of Modern Art acquired a stereolithography model of the original design in 2001. The sponsors of the Museum of Sex found a home for their concept in a former retail and office space in Manhattan, and opened their doors in 2002. (SHoP had no connection with that space.)

The Frank Gehry of prefab housing
The work of architect William Massie is another example of this new generation's pragmatic approach to the design-build process. With practical considerations very much in the vein of the SHoP approach, Massie has devised an approach that could bring customized design to the cash-strapped masses—an

approach that lead architectural critic Reed Kroloff to call Massie the "Frank Gehry of prefab housing."

What sets Bill Massie apart, Kroloff writes in *Esquire*, is his "bona fide Big Idea," his notion that architects should operate much closer to the building process. This notion is revolutionary, Kroloff explains, because of the disparate goals and seemingly irreconcilable differences between the goals and concerns of architects and the manufacturers of building materials:

You see, the building industry relies on standardization to minimize costs. Architects, on the other hand, tailor each project to their clients' needs. Customization costs more than off-the shelf. A lot more. The result: Architects design less than 10 percent of the houses in America, leaving most people to live in the cheaper, cookie-cutter world suburbia.

Indeed, Massie is so close to the manufacturing and construction side of the architectural equation that he has actually made some of the components of his designs himself, using his own computer-driven, laser cutting-and-milling machines

to sculpt Styrofoam forms that serve as molds for poured concrete. Massie incorporates concrete, cut steel, and other inexpensive materials into his designs to keep construction costs low.

It must be kept in mind that, although Massie is a doggedly down-to-earth designer, his goal is a rather lofty one: to use digital design technology to "redefine architectural practice and making." And although he's part of the newest generation of techno-focused architects, he sees the forms he creates on the computer as extensions of Modernism. In a 2002 interview, Massie told *Business Week*'s Thane Peterson:

What I'm trying to do is an extension of modernism [that goes back to] its true beginnings— when modernist homes were reasonably priced. If someone is thinking of building a typical suburban house, I can do an interesting modernist house instead for the same amount of money. People don't have to pay a huge premium to live in a beautiful and somewhat experimental space. The way light rakes across something curving is completely different from the way it strikes a flat wall.

One of SHoP's most blatantly biomorphic structures, the design of the Museum of Sex was inspired by the contours of the human body and would include a structural "skin" that would encase the building in translucent layers that peeled back in places to allow vertical movement or light filtration or to house displays.

Architect William Massie won the 2002 Museum of Modern Art/P.S.1 Contemporary Art Center Young Architects competition in New York—the same award that SHoP won with Dunescape, and which put both designers on the critics' radar. Massie's design was equally biomorphic, "blending the terms and associated ideas of surf, surface and sensuality as they relate to the natural landscape, the urban landscape, and the landscape of the body."

Urban beach

Interestingly, one of Massie's designs won the 2002 Museum of Modern Art/P.S.1 Contemporary Art Center Young Architects competition in New York—the same award that SHoP won with Dunescape, and which put both designers on the critics' radar. Massie's design was equally biomorphic. According to Massie, his work on Playa Urbana/Urban Beach began "from the conceptual basis of blending the terms and associated ideas of surf, surface and sensuality as they relate to the natural landscape, the urban landscape and the landscape of the body."

The museum described the project as a "highly graphic landscape that unites the site's natural and built elements and addresses concepts of surface and sensuality." Erected outdoors in P.S.1's 40,000-square-foot (12,200-square-meter) courtyard, the temporary installation incorporated wavelike structures made of PVC tubing that wound throughout the space to provide shade and shelter. The design included showers, a hot tub, and three rectangular reflecting/wading pools set above ground

and made of brightly colored polystyrene foam. Lined with rubberized truck-bed material in brilliant shades of green, pink, and yellow, the pools glowed at night. These pools were surrounded by a system of curved screens made of steel ribs that were laser-cut by the manufacturer directly from Massie's computer instructions.

In fact, all of the fabricated components of this project were spawned by Massie's computer-centric approach, which takes his design directly from the abstract, virtual design space to the concrete, real-world space of the fabrication facility. Explaining his process, Massie writes on his firm's website:

Our studio deconstructs the entire project in the computer, producing sections/drawings which are sent digitally to the laser-cutting facility to be fabricated with no other mediation. The pools are constructed in a similar fashion… with the use of a computer numerically controlled milling machine. The foam is then sprayed with a flexible plastic utilized in industrial processes such

as oil pipeline and truck-bed linings.

Big belt

Massie applied his evolving notions of the design-build process to the development and construction of his own home in the foothills of the Big Belt Mountains in Montana. (Massie Architecture maintains facilities in Bozeman, Montana, where Massie first hung out his own shingle, but also has offices in New York City and Troy, New York.) He describes the so-called Big Belt House as "the first full-scale iteration of seven years of on-going research in which a constant effort to bridge virtual and corporally occupiable space is achieved." In 2000, Massie received a Progressive Architecture award for the house.

Massie designed the flat-roofed, buff-colored house to fit naturally into the surrounding landscape. His guiding design concept was the idea of "visual rhyming," which Massie saw as an "attempt to develop a relationship to the landscape that is less object/subject in nature." He talked about the project in 2002 with Thane Peterson:

I worked a lot of this out in the Big Belt House in the Big Belt Mountains, which is my own house. It's a huge experiment—a series of buildings funded by my wife, me, my family, my friends, the bank, and everyone else. One of the things I did there was take a global positioning survey and digitally map the site so I knew every curve of the ground exactly. I took the computer model and based the design of the house on the geometry of the site so it kind of blends into the landscape. It's quite fascinating.

For this design, Massie literally took the lay of the land, what he called "foreground topographies," and mapped them to the computer, where they were "digitally reassembled" to form the space of the building. The "visual rhyme," then, was this influence of the external on the internal, the reflection of the natural forms of the landscape in the abstract, computer-generated forms of the house. "This idea of rhyming attempts to assimilate the building with the landscape," Massie has written, "but does not attempt to approximate the landscape. Visual rhyming is not an idea of camouflage, instead, as in 'cat' and 'hat' there exists an auditory similarity binding together two disparate words. In the same way, an imposed spatial construct and a natural landscape are bound together by distinct visual similarities."

He describes the linear courtyard along the eastern side of the house as an "ante-building" that approximated the size and shape of the building's interior and enhanced its relationship to the site by "creating controlled exterior space which mediates between the landscape and the enclosed interior space."

Significantly, Massie created no blueprints for Big Belt House. The computer files were accessed directly by a Computer Numerically Controlled (CNC) milling machine, which created approximately 1,500 individual pieces of rigid foam. These foam pieces were assembled, Massie writes, "like a child's puzzle." The puzzle pieces became the formwork in which reinforced, poured-in-place portal frames were created onsite.

Big sky

Big Belt House was an exploration of the possibilities of a design strategy that blended the complex curvatures of a landscape with the form of the building erected on it. Massie's Big Sky House looked at an opposite notion, the idea of "marking" the landscape, of erecting a structure that would become a kind of "signpost in a landscape devoid of manmade registration."

Easily one of Massie's most striking designs, Big Sky House, which was developed for a British couple as a Broadwater County, Montana, vacation home, is a four-story, 2,000-square-foot (600-square-meter), metal-clad, silver tower that rises up from an expansive plain. The north and south walls of the house consist mostly of windows, which allow the landscape to show through the building.

Massie positioned Big Sky House so that it would appear to mark the end of the country road along which it is located. The house is visible from a distance of six miles (9.7km) to drivers traveling west on Highway 12 toward Townsend, Montana.

According to Massie, the only comparable structure within an hour's drive is the sign for a local Exxon station. The highway eventually curves around Mount Edith, changing the relationship between the road and the building, adding an element of movement to the design.

Getting the house into exactly the right position relative to the highway was critical to the success of Massie's concept. Massie writes, "This building marks and measures the landscape by being positioned critically in relation to two significant landscape features: the straight line of the highway and the obstacle of the mountain. Through its precise siting, the building mediates between subject and object."

To "achieve the perfect alignment necessary for the building to create the desired result," Massie reportedly cut and assembled the building's plywood foundation forms full-size in his shop, and then assembled them on the site so that he could make incremental adjustments before the concrete was poured. He was able literally to pick up the assembled formwork and move it around until he was satisfied with the placement. Massie reportedly used his CNC milling machine to create the forms for the curving windows, fire-rated beam covers, closets, kitchen cabinets, and interior walls of the house.

Big box

A third experimental project, Massie's House for a Photographer, tested a design scheme that Massie characterized as "a modern approach, but not a modernist strategy." The theme here is the separation of landscape and building, and it was inspired, according to Massie, by the client's photographs of industrial buildings, commercial structures, boxcars, and tractor-trailers. "These somewhat primitive/modern 'containers' and their relationship to the landscape were the stimulus of this project's approach," he writes.

By design, the rectilinear, "blaze orange" house stands in stark contrast to the open field in which it stands. Massie writes:

The hunter wears a blaze orange hunting hat or coat to distinguish him/herself from the natural landscape, further distinguishing him/herself from the hunted. This "alien" color further emphasizes the disconnection between the building and the rural/suburban culture and allows for a clear reading of the dwelling—as that of a primitive structure.

The building is constructed of poured-in-place concrete, insulated on the exterior with a composite, rigid-foam-and-Ferrocement fiberboard, which gives it its dissonant hue. Massie utilized CNC milling equipment to prefabricate some components of the house, including entry and bedroom partitions.

The shape and color of the building are intended to disconnect the structure from its rural setting. The house has a "somewhat alien politic" that Massie underscores literally with a unique visual effect: by design, the building appears to hover 18 inches (46 centimeters) above the ground.

sources

Chapter 1: Birth of the blob:
Postwar architects and designers rage against the machine age

Eidelberg, Martin, and Paul Johnson (editors): *Design 1935–1965, What Modern Was: Selections from the Liliane and David M. Stewart Collection*, Harry N Abrams, 2001.

"Frank Lloyd Wright," *The Architectural Forum*, January 1948.

Gossel, Peter, and Gabriele Leuthauser: *Architecture in the Twentieth Century*, Taschen America Llc, 1999.

Keintz, Renee: "The Power of Wright: Mid-century designer's vision shapes modern home front," *Houston Chronicle*, February 8, 2002.

Kerr, Ann: *Collector's Encyclopedia of Russel Wright*, 2nd edition, Collector Books, 2002.

Kirkham, Pat: *Charles and Ray Eames: Designers of the Twentieth Century*, MIT Press, 1998.

Kostof, Spiro: *A History of Architecture, Settings and Rituals*, Oxford University Press, 1985.

Lapidus, Morris: *Too Much Is Never Enough: An Autobiography by Morris Lapidus*, Rizzoli International Publications, 1996.

Pina, Leslie: *Fifties Furniture*, Schiffer Publishing, Ltd., 1996.

Sharp, Dennis: *Twentieth Century Architecture: A Visual History*, Facts on File, Inc., 1991.

Sharp, Dennis: *The Illustrated Encyclopedia of Architects and Architecture*, Quatro Publishing, 1991.

Steen, Karen E: "The Playful Search for Beauty," *Metropolis*, January 2001.

Stewart, Doug: "Cheese Holes, Blobs and Woggles," *Smithsonian*, February 2002.

Wright, Sylvia Hart: *Sourcebook of Contemporary North American Architecture: From Postwar to Postmodern*, Van Nostrand Reinhold, 1989.

Chapter 2: Blob's your uncle:
Frank O. Gehry shows a generation how to design outside the box

Abrams, Janet, Karen Nichols, Lisa
Burke, Patrick Burke (editors):
*Michael Graves : Buildings and
Projects 1990–1994*, Rizzoli, 1995.

Art and Culture,
http://www.artandculture.com/

Blanchard, Tamsin, and Deyan
Sudjic: "Designer Living," *The
Observer*, March 31, 2002.

Boissiere, Olivier and Martin Filler:
*The Vitra Design Museum: Frank
Gehry Architect*, Rizzoli International
Publications, 1990.

Busch, Akiko: *The Photography of
Architecture: Twelve Views*, Van
Nostrand Reinhold, 1993.

Case Scheer, Brenda: "Aronoff
Addition—A Field Guide to Meta-
Narratives," *ArchitectureWeek*,
January 3, 2001.

"CATIA at Frank O. Gehry & Associates, Inc.", a case study published
by CenitDesktop, 2002.

Chollet, Laurence B: *The Essential
Frank O. Gehry*, Harry N Abrams,
2001.

Contemporary Architects, Macmillan
Reference Books, 1980.

Dal Co, Francesco, and Kurt W.
Forster: *Frank O. Gehry: The
Complete Works*, The Monacelli
Press, 1998.

Dobney, Stephen (editor): *Michael
Graves: Selected and Current
Works*, August 1999.

Emmons, Jasen: "Am I Experienced?" *Slate*, March 16, 2001.

Enlow, Clair: "Frank Gehry Rock
Temple," *ArchitectureWeek*,
July 12 2000.

Fiske, Diane M: "VSBA Exhibition,"
ArchitectureWeek, June 27, 2001.

Forgey, Benjamin: "Pitch Out the T
Square: Computer Design Tools
Have Taken Architecture From Plane
to Fancy," *Washington Post*, March
3, 2001.

Frishberg, Manny: "The Blob:
Seattle's Music Edifice," *Wired*,
June 20, 2000.

Garcetti, Gil, Frank O. Gehry: *Iron:
Erecting the Walt Disney Concert
Hall*, Princeton Architectural Press,
October 2002.

Giovannini, Joseph: "Franks, a Lot,"
New York Magazine, May 28, 2001.

Heyer, Paul: *American Architecture:
Ideas and Ideologies in the Late
Twentieth Century*, Van Nostrand
Reinhold, 1993.

Huck, Peter: "The Gehry Effect," F2
Network, www.f2.com.au/ Decem
ber 13, 2001.

Jencks, Charles: *The New Paradigm
in Architecture*, Yale University
Press, 2002.

Lacayo, Richard: "The Frank Gehry
Experience," *Time Europe*,
September 18, 2000.

Lasere, Arthur, "Guggenheim
Museum Bilbao—Frank O. Gehry,"
Culturevulture.com, May 30, 2001.

Libby, Brian: "Reevaluating Post-
modernism, " *ArchitectureWeek*,
Jun 5, 2002.

Marshall, Alex: "How to Make a
Frank Gehry Building," *The New
York Times Magazine*, April 8, 2001.

Matthews, Kevin: *The Great
Buildings Collection on CD-ROM*,
Artifice, 2001.

Novitski, B.J.: "A.I.A. Announces
Highest Honors," *ArchitectureWeek*,
January 3, 2001.

"Resurrecting Dresden Cathedral,"
Architecture, June 1997.

Sharp, Dennis: *The Illustrated
Encyclopedia of Architects and
Architecture*, Quatro Publishing,
1991.

Stein, Karen D: "Frank Gehry's
Dream Project—The Guggenheim
Museum Bilbao draws the world
to Spain's Basque Country,"
Architectural Record, October, 1997.

Stattaford, Andrew: "Are You Experi-
enced? In Seattle, A Big-Bucks
Tribute to Rock 'N' Roll," *NRO
Weekend*, August 26–27, 2000.

Taub, Eric: "Architects Grow Reliant
on the 40 Pound Pencil—The
Computer," *New York Times*,
August 10, 2000.

Templer, Karen: "Frank Gehry," *Salon*, October 5, 1999.

Van Bruggen, Coosje, and Frank O. Gehry: *Frank O. Gehry: Guggenheim Museum Bilbao*, Solomon R. Guggenheim Museum, March 1998.

Weisberg, Jacob: "Give That Man Another Guggenheim!" *Slate*, December 6, 1998.

Worsley, Giles: "How to build the new world", *Telegraph*, March 18, 2000.

Chapter 3: New tools of the trade: Information-age architects and designers animate the process

Birn, Jeremy: "High-end 3D Animation and Rendering Software," 3dRender.com, 2002.

Blinn, J: "A Generalization of Algebraic Surface Drawing," *ACM Transactions on Graphics*, July, 1982.

Bozdoc, Marian: *The History of CAD*, iMB 2002.

Computer Desktop Encyclopedia, The Computer Language Co. Inc., 2002.

Doyle, Claire F: *Videography*, PSN Publications, 1992.

Lynn, Greg, *Animate Form*, Princeton Architectural Press, 1998.

Menon, J: "An Introduction to Implicit Techniques," *SIGGRAPH Course Notes on Implicit Surfaces for Geometric Modeling and Computer Graphics*, 1996.

Rashid, Karim: *Karim Rashid: I Want to Change the World*, Universal Books, March 2002.

Safire, William: "On Language— Defenestration," *New York Times*, December 1, 2002.

Stille, Alexander: "Invisible Cities," *Lingua Franca*, July/August 1998.

Valentino, James, and Joseph Goldberg: *Introduction to Computer Numerical Control*, Prentice Hall, 2001.

Wyvill, G., C. McPhetters, and B. Wyvill: "Data Structure for Soft Objects," *The Visual Computer*, 1986.

Walker, John (editor): *The Autodesk File: Bits of History, Words of Experience*, Que, July 1989.

Ward, Matthew: "An Overview of Metaballs/Blobby Objects," *Worcester Polytechnic Institute*, March 1997.

Chapter 4: A blob by any other name: Greg Lynn creates a manifesto for a new architectonic philosophy

Bergen, Ann: "The Easier Beauty of Animate Form," *Architectural Record*, November 2000.

"Blobs: Why Technics is Square and Topology is Groovy," *Any*, May 1996.

Dery, Mark: "Soft House: Home Grown," *ArtByte*, November–December 2000.

Giovannini, Joseph: "Korean Church," Akropolis.net, 2000.

Jana, Reena: "Designing a Home for Digital Arts," *Wired*, August 9, 2000.

Kristal, Marc: "Measuring the Competition," *Metropolis*, November 2002.

Lacayo, Richard: "You Could Call Him Mr. Softee," Time.com

Lynn, Greg: *Animate Form*, Princeton Architectural Press, 1999.

Lynn, Greg: *Folds, Bodies & Blobs: Collected Essays*, La Lettre Volee, 1998.

Muschamp, Herbert: "A Queens Factory Is Born Again as a Church," *New York Times*, 1999.

Muschamp, Herbert, "Architecture's Claim on the Future: The Blob," *New York Times*, July 23, 2000.

Oser, Alan: "From a Laundry to a Perfume Factory to a Church," *New York Times*, July 28, 1996.

Taub, Eric, "Architects Grow Reliant on the 40-Pound Pencil—the Computer," *New York Times*, August 10, 2000.

Chapter 5: Biological thinking: Architects propagate a biomorphic aesthetic

Binet, Helene: *Architecture of Zaha Hadid in Photographs*, Lars Muller Publishers, 2001.

Byars, Mel: *On/Off: New Electronic Products*, Universe Books, 2001.

Cohen, Preston Scott: *Contested Symmetries and other Predicaments in Architecture*, Princeton Architectural Press, February 2001.

Crosbie, Michael J: "Norman Foster: Analog and Digital Ecology," *ArchitecturWeek*, September 20, 2000.

Curtis, William J. R., and Balkrishna Doshi: *Balkrishna Doshi: An Architecture for India*, Rizzoli International Publications, 1988.

Davidson, Adam: "Revolution from Without," *Metropolis*, February/March 1999.

Gardiner, Virginia: "It's Hip Not to Be Square" *Dwell*, May 2003.

Hales, Linda: "Blobs, Pods and People" *Washington Post*, March 25, 2001.

Hadid, Zaha, and Aaron Betsky: *Zaha Hadid: The Complete Buildings and Projects*, Rizzoli International Publications, 1998.

He Herington, Peter, and Libby Brooks: "Giant Bubble by Thames Will Be Home to London's New Leaders," *The Guardian*, February 27, 1999.

Imperial, Alicia: "New Flatness: Surface Tension in Digital Architecture," *Birdhouse*, 2000.

"Inside London's New 'Glass Egg,'" *BBC News*, July 16, 2002.

Jencks, Charles: *The New Paradigm in Architecture: The Language of Post-Modernism*, Yale University Press, 2002.

Pearman, Hugh: "Norman Foster and his incredible wobbling bridge," *The Sunday Times*, London, June 18, 2000.

Prestinenza Puglisi, Luigi: *Hyperarchitecture: Spaces in the Electronic Age*, Birkhauser, 1999.

Schwartz, Ineke: "A Testing Ground for Interactivity," *Archis*, September 1997.

Sharp, Dennis: *The Illustrated Encyclopedia of Architects and Architecture*, Quatro Publishing, 1991.

Steele, James: *Rethinking Modernism for the Developing World: The Complete Architecture of Balkrishna Doshi*, Watson-Guptill Publications, 1998.

Sudjic, Deyan: "The Thriller on the River," *The Observer*, May 5, 2002.

Usher, Rod: "Better Late...," *Time*, October 21, 2002.

Worsley, Giles: "Why Foster Hasn't Cracked it," *Telegraph*, April 7, 2002.

Chapter 6: An utterance without a language: Hani Rashid and Lise Anne Couture find a new architecture in the "dimension-less territories"

"American Notes, Los Angeles: Monumental Folly," *Time*, December 19, 1988.

Amorosi, A.D: "Brother Where Art Thou? Hani and Karim Rashid Find Union," *CityPaper.net*, December 6–13, 2001.

Andia, Alfredo, and Claudia Busch: "Architects Design in Cyberspace and Real Space for the NYSE," *The Architecture of Cyberspace*, August 1999.

Keegan, Edward: "Knoll's A3 System Workstation," *Metropolis*, June 11, 2002.

Borins, Sara: "They've Got Designs on the Future," *National Post*, August 80, 2002.

Costello, Laura: "Steel Cloud to Hang Over L.A. Freeway," National Building Museum website http://www.nbm.org.

"Cyberspace, Guggenheim Virtual Museum, Asymptote Architects," *Arcspace* July 22, 2001.

Giblin, P.J.: "What Is an Asymptote?" *Mathematics Gazette*, 1972.

Gray, A.: "Using Mathematica to Find Asymptotic Curves," *Modern Differential Geometry of Curves and Surfaces with Mathematica*, Second Edition, CRC Press, 1997.

Hill, John: "Steel Cloud," A Weekly Dose of Architecture, http://www.archidose.org/May99/050399.htm/

Moreno, Shonquis: "Blurred Vision," *Frame Magazine*, Sept/Oct 2002.

"NYSE Installs '3D Trading Floor,'" *VR News*, April 1999.

Rashid, Hani, and Lise Anne Couture: *Asymptote: Architecture at the Interval*, Rizzoli International Publications, August 1995.

Rashid, Hani, and Lise Anne Couture: *Asymptote: Flux*, Phaidon Press Inc., June 2002.

Silberman, Steve: "Interesting 3D/VRML App for Wall Street," *Reuters*, September 18, 1998.

Spingarn-Koff, Jason: "Guggenheim Going Virtual," *Wired*, June 9, 2000.

Chapter 7: The "poster boy" for blobism: Karim Rashid sets out to change the world

Betsky, Aaron: "Soft Focus: New York Designer Karim Rashid Wants to Change the Way You Feel," *Wired*, January 2001.

Blair, Dike: "3 Stores/3 Chairs: Looking For A Modern Modern," *ArtByte*, Summer 1999.

Branwyn, Gareth: "Millennium Jargon—A Bushel of Buzzwords for the New New Economy," *TechTV*, March 6, 2001.

Brinkley, Rob: "Curves ahead: Karim Rashid Transforms Mundane Objects," *The Dallas Morning News*, March 18, 2002.

Clewley, Robin: "Art That Makes You Say Hmmm," *Wired*, March 7, 2001.

Daspin, Eileen, and June Fletcher, "Top Designers Pick Haute Products," WSJ.coml, http://homes.wsj.com/housegarden/indoorliving/20000301-daspin.html

Gibney, Frank, Jr., and Belinda Liscombe: "the World is Wild About Fine Design," *Time*, July 31, 2000.

Hall, Peter: "The Rashid Machine, *Metropolis*, February 2001.

Hill, Logan: "Karim Rashid—Design Chairman," *New York Magazine*, 1999.

Hine, Thomas: "Looking Alive: The objects around us are becoming more like living things," *Atlantic*, November 2001.

"Interior Design Asks Karim Rashid," *Interior Design*, February 11, 2003.

Muschamp, Herbert: "A Humble Manhole Cover Conveys the Global Grid," *New York Times*, September 26, 1999.

Patton, Phil: "The Little Can That Could," *New York Times*, September 3, 1998.

Patton, Phil: "From Eureka to Your House—The Evolution of a $50 Chair," *New York Times*, December 10, 1998.

"Plastics Help Designers Think Out of Traditional Design Box," *Time*, April 2000.

Rashid, Karim: *Karim Rashid: I Want to Change the World*, Universal Books, March 2002.

Roane, Kit R: "For Stylish Millennium Official Manhole Cover," *New York Times*, September 16, 1999.

Rude, Kelly: "Rashid introduces rearrangeable furniture system," *Interiors*, March/April 2001.

Snowden Picket, Lynn: "Object Lesson—Karim Rashid is on a mission to teach the entire world an object lesson," *ONE*, September 2001.

Stalford, Maria: "Injection Molded Fun at Rice Gallery," *Thresher*, February 2, 2001.

Stein, Jeannine, "Redesign Upends Old Soap Dish, *Los Angeles Times*, September 28, 2002.

Sterling, Bruce: "Blobjects & Biodesign," http://www.artbyte.com/shared/articles/blobjects/blobject.html/

Sterling, Bruce and Peter Lewis: "All About Gadgets and Gizmosity," *Fortune*, February 2001.

Tadic, Natalia: "Karim Rashid—Remarkable Designer," *Canoe*, January 27, 2001.

Wadler, Joyce: "Hipster Goes With the Flow in Life and Art," *New York Times*, January 18, 2000.

Webb, Michael: "Biomorphic Rainbow," *Frame Magazine*, May/June, 2002.

Chapter 8: Outside the beige box: Device designers shake hands with the blob

Allbritton, Chris: "MAC-stravaganza: Apple's new product line is more polished than ever," *Associated Press*, July 23, 2000.

Arthur, Charles: "Son of iMac," *Independent News*, January 14, 2002.

Dawkins, Richard: *The Selfish Gene*, Oxford University Press, 1990.

Ellis, Michael: "Retro Reality: Modern design evokes a more nostalgic spirit," *Reuters*, January 8, 2003.

Fried, Ian: "New iMac 'Less Shocking' Than Original," *CNET*, January 8, 2002.

Garratt, Sheryl: "Technology Innovator: Jonathan Ives, Designer of the iMac," *The Observer*, March 31, 2002.

George, Wes: "The iMac: A Case Study in Historical Contingency & Evolutionary Convergence," *The Mac Observer*, August 21, 2000.

Gore, Andrew: "The Vision Thing: Defying Gravity... Again," *Macworld*, July 1998.

Kelley, Tom, with Jonathan Littman: *The Art of Innovation*, Doubleday, January 2001.

Lachapelle, Marc: "Car Dreams Come True," *The Toronto Star*, February 21, 1998.

Lachapelle, Marc: "Wheels: The Bug's Back—Invisible Man Who Brought It To You," *Guardian*, June 22, 1998.

Manjoo, Farhad: "iMac: What's in a Design, Anyway?" *Wired*, January 11, 2002.

McClellan, Jim: "Chips with Everything," *The Observer*, March 31, 2002.

McLeod, Kate: *Beetlemania: The Story of the Car That Captured the Hearts of Millions*, Smithmark Publishing 1999.

Myerson, Jeremy: *IDEO—Masters of Innovation*, te Neues Publishing Company, May 2001.

Nauman, Matt: "VW Beetle Injects Charisma Into Industry," *San Jose Mercury News*, December 21, 1998.

Needleman, Rafe: "Bye-bye, Beige," *Red Herring*, July 1999.

Nickell, Joe: "Edsel or Etch-a-Sketch?" *Wired*, August 13, 1998.

Patton, Phil: *Bug: The Strange Mutations of the World's Most Famous Automobile*, Simon & Schuster 2002.

Parks, Bob: "Deconstructing Cute," *Business 2.0*, December 2002.

Pelletier, Joel: "Apple Design Group Redefines Computing," *AD Times Design*, May 12, 1998.

Rettie, John: "VW's Freeman Thomas: an underrated star designer," *Ward's Auto World*, May 1999.

Scott-Joynt, Jeremy: "Apple's Flat-Screen Hopes," *BBC News Online*, January 8, 2002.

Sterling, Bruce: "Blobjects & Biodesign," http://www.artbyte.com/shared/articles/blobjects/blobject.html/

Zager, Marsha: "The Smart Money Behind Computer Aesthetics," *NewsFactor.com*, December 2002.

Chapter 9: Next generation:
The post-blobists get real

Forgey, Benjamin: "Pitch Out the T Square: Computer Design Tools Have Taken Architecture From Plane to Fancy," *Washington Post*, March 3, 2001.

Giovannini, Joseph: "The Inn Crowd," *New York Magazine*, August 21, 2000.

Giovannini, Joseph: "Digitally inclined: Shifting the architectural model," *Red Herring*, December 2000.

Hawthorne, Christopher: "SHoP Talk," *Metropolis*, May 2001.

Jencks, Charles: *The New Paradigm in Architecture: The Language of Post-Modernism*, Yale University Press, 2002.

Kroloff, Reed: "The Architect: William Massie," *Esquire*, December 2002.

Ringen, Jonathan: "Bridging the Divide: SHoP's Pedestrian Bridge Is a Lesson on Rebuilding Lower Manhattan," *Metropolis*, July 2002.

Sciaudone, Christiana: "Museum Of Sex Draws The Curious On First Day," *Newsday*, October 6, 2002.

SHoP/Sharples Holden Pasquarelli (guest editors): *Versioning: Evolutionary Techniques in Architecture*, Josey-Bass, December 2002.

Peterson, Thane: "Daring, Modernist Homes on the Cheap," *Business Week*, June 18, 2002.

Photographer credits

Courtesy of Asymtote Architects/www.asymptote-
architecture.com, 102; 105; 106; 109; 111; 113;
114; 115; 117; 118
Movie poster for *The Blob*, Allied Artists, (1958), 9
Duncan Brinsmead/Courtesy of Alias|Wavefront, 61
Richard Bryant/www.arcaid.co.uk, 94; 95
Courtesy of Discreet/www.discreet.com, 51
Thomas Dix/Vitra Design Museum, 33; 38
© 2003 Eames Office/www.eamesoffice.com, 21 (left);
22 (left)
© Erika Barahona Ede, Guggenheim Bilbao, 30; 42; 43;
45; 46
Julie Flohr/Garofalo Architects/
www.garofalo.a-node.net, 101
Courtesy of Greg Lynn FORM/www.glform.com, 10; 65;
66; 67; 69; 70; 73; 74; 76; 77; 78; 79; 80; 81; 82;
84; 85
Hunter Freeman/Apple Computer, Inc., 147
Courtesy of Gehry Partners LLP, 34; 41
© David Heald/Solomon R. Guggenheim Museum,
New York, 14; 15
Courtesy of Herman Miller, Inc./www.hermanmiller.com,
21 (right)
Courtesy of Ideo/www.ideo.com, 148; 155
Courtesy of the Institute of Contemporary Art,
New York/www.ps1.org, 171
Courtesy of KD Lab/Discreet/www.discreet.com,
62 (right)
Courtesy of Knoll/www.knoll.com, 25; 27
Courtesy of Kolatan MacDonald/
www.kolatanmacdonaldstudio.com 88, 89; 90; 91
Mark Laita/Apple Computer, Inc./www.apple.com, 4;
144; 157
Benedict Luxmoore/www.arcaid.co.uk, 86; 93
Lyon Convergences-Cultural Centre for Lyon, France,
Polygone Studio, Montreal, Quebec,Canada/
www.polygonestudio.com, 52; 53; 54; 55
Courtesy of the Moma Design Store, Museum of Modern
Art, New York/www.momastore.org, 23; 24

© Michael Moran Photography/Kolatan Macdonald, 87
Courtesy of the National CorvetteMuseum/
www.corvettemuseum.com, 28
Courtesy of Platigue Image & TomekBaginski/Discreet/
www.discreet.com, 62 (bottom left)
Pleasurscape, 2001 Commission, Rice University Art
Gallery/ www.ruf.rice.edu/~ruag/index1.html, 136
Dan Pressman/Courtesy of Alias|Wavefront/
www.aliaswavefront.com, 58; 59; 60
Courtesy of Karim Rashid, Inc./www.karimrashid.com,
124; 126; 127; 128; 129; 130; 131; 132; 133; 135
Courtesy of St. Louis Chamber of Commerce/
www.stlrcga.org, 12
Phil Schaafsma/Courtesy of Herman Miller, Inc., 6; 13;
18; 20; 22 (right)
Courtesy of SHoP, Sharples, Holden, Pasquarelli/
www.shoparc.com, 159; 160; 161; 163; 165;
166; 169
Softscape, 2001, San Francisco Museum of Modern
Art/www.sfmoma.org, 137
Courtesy of Philippe Starck/www.philippe-starck.com,
151; 152; 153
Lara Swimmer/© 2000 By Experience Music Project, 48
Lara Swimmer & Stanley Swimmer/© 2000
Experience Music Project, 49
©Jason Szenes/Corbis Sygma, 41
Images generated with OpenDX, Courtesy of Matt Ward/
www.cs.wpi.edu/~matt/courses/cs563/talks/metaballs.html,
56; 57
Courtesy of Umbra/www.umbra.com, 120; 123; 183
Courtesy of UnchartedTerritory/Discreet/
www.discreet.com, 62 (top left)
Katsuhisa Kida/Ushida Findlay, 96; 97
Courtesy of Volkswagen of America/www.vw.com, 2; 3;
139; 140; 143
Courtesy of Zaha Hadid Architects/
www.zahahadid.com, 98; 99

Acknowledgments

Writers face the blank screen alone, but no one creates a book without help; I had lots of it on this project. To all the hard-working professionals at Rockport Publishers who shared with me their time and talent, I want to offer my heartfelt thanks. I'd especially like to mention the contributions of.

Josh Brackett, copyeditor extraordinaire, whose knowledge and judgment provided a much needed editorial safety net for this project. Pros of your caliber are becoming a rarity in this business, I'm sad to say. Thanks for keeping me from looking like an idiot in print.

Betsy Gammons, peerless photo editor, without whose hard work and stubborn resourcefulness this book would have been half as beautiful—and a third as much fun to write. For your warm encouragement, your frank sense of humor, and your indefatigable ability to shrug off one setback after another, I thank you.

Paula Munier, senior editor, writer, and friend, who came up with the idea for this project and thought of me. Without your unflagging faith and support, I simply could not have written this book.

I'd also like to acknowledge some special people who helped us with our photo hunt. Many, many thanks to Tom Wegehaupt at Volkswagen America, Jackilin Hah at Greg Lynn FORM; Christin Minnotte at Asymptote Architects; Jade Seto and Chris Barnes at Umbra; Kim Bush at the Solomon R. Guggenheim Museum in New York; Erika Barahona Ede at the Guggenheim Museum in Bilbao, Spain; Alexander von Vegesack at the Vitra Design Museum; Sue Runfola at Apple Computer; Alexandra Yessios at formZ; LeiLei Sun at Alias/Wavefront; Lynn Winter and Whitney Mortimer at IDEO; Manon Janssens at Zaha Hadid Architects; Lindsay Stewart at Access Communications; Julie Fauteux at Discreet; Kazumi Koseko at Ushida Findlay; Tanya Berkin, consultant to Discreet; Danielle Lamothe at SGI; Rachael Dorsey at P.S.1 Contemporary Art Center in New York; Keith Mendenhall and Laura Stella at Gehry Partners, LLP; Lynnel Herrera at Karim Rashid Inc.; digital design maven Matthew Ward; and Dana Sobya at CHE Library, who tracked down an obscure article that I just couldn't live without.

I'd also like to thank the design team at Wilson Harvey of London; Rockport's own incomparable senior designer, Regina Grenier; and our overworked but not underappreciated (by me, at least) art coordinator, Cora Hawks, for their exceptional work on this book.

Folks, I couldn't have done it without you.

John K. Waters
March 2003

About the author

John K. Waters is a freelance journalist who has covered the technology beat from Silicon Valley for more than 15 years. He is senior correspondent for *Application Development Trends* magazine and a contributing editor for *Programmer's Report*. He is also the author of more than a dozen books, including *John Chambers and the Cisco Way: Managing Through Volatility* (John Wiley & Sons, 2002) and the *Everything Computer Book* (Adams Media Corporation, 2000). He lives in Palo Alto, California. (Photo by Mardeene Mitchell.)